S0-AWZ-279

.92092
MULFORD
1992e

973
.92092
MULFORD
1992

ELIZABETH DOLE

Public Servant

Carolyn Mulford

Library Resource Center
Renton Technical College
3000 NE 4th St.
Renton, WA 98056-4195

—Contemporary Women Series—

ENSLOW PUBLISHERS, INC.

Bloy St. and Ramsey Ave.	P.O. Box 38
Box 777	Aldershot
Hillside, N.J. 07205	Hants GU12 6BP
U.S.A.	U.K.

Copyright © 1992 by Carolyn Mulford

All rights reserved.

No part of this book may be reproduced by any means
without the written permission of the publisher.

Library of Congress Cataloging-In-Publication Data

Mulford, Carolyn.
  Elizabeth Dole, public servant / Carolyn Mulford.
    p. cm. — (Contemporary women series)
  Includes bibliographical references (p.) and index.
  Summary: A biography of the current president of the American Red Cross
from her childhood in North Carolina through her years of public service in
Washington, DC.
    ISBN 0-89490-331-4
    1. Dole, Elizabeth Hanford—Juvenile literature. 2. Cabinet
officers—United States—Biography—Juvenile literature. [1. Dole,
 Elizabeth Hanford. 2. Cabinet officers. 3. American Red Cross.]
I. Title. II. Series.
E840.8.D63M85 1992
973.92'092—dc20
[B]   91-25395
                                                      CIP
                                                      AC
Printed in the United States of America

10 9 8 7 6 5 4 3 2 1

Illustration Credits:

American Red Cross, p. 131; Beardsley Ruml, II, *Harvard Law School Yearbook: 1965*, p.
47; Boyden High School *Yellow Jacket*, pp. 28,32; Courtesy of Elizabeth Dole, pp. 14, 15,
25, 36, 66, 67; Department of Labor, pp. 8, 116; Department of Transportation, pp. 88, 90,
96, 100; James P. Barringer, Jr., *Salisbury Post*, p. 72; *Salisbury Post*, p. 17; U.S. Senate,
pp. 97, 102, 113; White House, p. 109.

Cover Illustration:

Globe Photos, Inc.

To the memory of
Lena Dunkin Mulford
and to
Mary Cathey Hanford,
two women who encouraged and supported their
daughters/friends as they followed unknown and
unexpected paths.

Acknowledgements

Many people have helped in the preparation of this book, and I wish to thank a few whose efforts were key. Foremost, Elizabeth Dole made time in her heavy schedule for interviews, gave me access to her speech and photo files, and asked her family and her staff members at the Department of Labor and the American Red Cross to assist with this project.

The Hanford family spent many hours with me. Mary Cathey Hanford provided invaluable assistance through her recollections and scrapbooks. She and her son, John Van Hanford II, led me to old friends in Salisbury and elsewhere who shared memories of Elizabeth as she was growing up. Among them were Jean Stanback Brumley, Betty Dan Nicholas Gilliam, Harold Isenberg, Elaine Richards, Julian and Blanche Robertson, and Fred Stanback. Several staff members of the *Salisbury Post* were also very helpful. In Washington, John Van Hanford III and Robin Dole contributed information.

A number of other Washingtonians gave insights into Elizabeth Dole's career. Among them were Tim Burr, Suzanne Rodgers Bush, and Charlotte Coffield.

A special thanks to Joyce Campbell, who read the manuscript with an eye for what students would want to know and endured hours of conversation about the book.

Carolyn Mulford

Contents

Elizabeth Dole

1

Madam Secretary

Limousines came down Capitol Hill and from Pennsylvania Avenue, bringing the president, senators, representatives, and business and labor leaders to the Frances Perkins Department of Labor Building. In the packed Great Hall, they sat on chairs and bleachers, touching elbows with government employees, family members, and friends.

They all came to see Elizabeth Hanford Dole take the oath of office as secretary of labor on January 30, 1989. An old friend and Harvard Law School classmate, now a judge, read the oath, while a new friend, a Job Corps trainee, held the Bible. Speaking quickly and with the Southern accent of her North Carolina childhood, the slender, dark-haired, hazel-eyed woman promised to carry out her duties.

Standing with them during the ceremony were President George Bush, her boss, and Senator Robert J. Dole, her husband. Less than a year before, Senator Dole, with his wife's assistance, had battled George Bush for the right to be the Republican candidate for president.

Probably not one person there doubted that Secretary Dole

would work hard to manage well the department's 18,500 employees and $31 billion budget. After all, she had been known for her diligence and dedication, what she called her perfectionism, from her first job as a civil servant in Washington, D.C., in 1966. She had worked her way up through a series of increasingly important jobs, the last one being secretary of transportation. In meetings of high-level staff, she had often been the only woman.

In her new position she would face many challenges. She would need wide and deep knowledge, skill in working with Congress and special interest groups, creativity, and persistence. Facing her were such national problems as preparing dropouts for good jobs, retraining workers in aging industries to make products to compete on the world market, making jobs as safe as possible, curbing the rising violation of child labor laws, bringing together battling unions and company owners, and giving women and minorities equal job opportunities. She would also deal with international problems, particularly in Eastern Europe.

When the Great Hall cleared and the limousines pulled away, Madam Secretary went to the cafeteria to meet and shake hands with staff members. This simple gesture symbolized her philosophy of respecting and working with people of all levels in Washington, but it sprang from lessons she learned as a child and young adult.

The woman President Bush had chosen for this difficult job had been preparing for it since she was a small child. In grade school Elizabeth, known as Liddy, organized—and ran—clubs for her classmates. In high school "Likeable Liddy" campaigned for—and usually won—offices in local and regional organizations.

When Liddy Hanford entered Duke University in 1954, she surprised her parents by majoring in political science and international affairs rather than home economics. The young woman already had decided she would not limit herself to doing what was then called women's work. Unlike most of her friends, she decided not to get married when she graduated.

"I just wasn't quite ready for that," she says. "There were things I wanted to do. I wasn't ready to settle down. I wanted to travel; I wanted to live in another part of the country; I wanted to work; I wanted to go to graduate school."

Having done all that and much more, she looks back and says, "It's interesting, because you don't know why you're listening to the beat of another drummer."

The beat sounded as the civil rights and women's movements began to demand equal opportunities for everyone in education and work. She benefited from the new laws and attitudes as she achieved higher and higher positions in government. At the same time, she worked hard to help others break through the "glass ceiling," the invisible barrier that keeps talented women and members of minority groups from rising to top positions.

Then, on October 24, 1990, after twenty-five years in government service and not quite two years as secretary of labor, she called Department of Labor employees into the Great Hall to tell them that she had resigned. In early 1991 she would become president of the American Red Cross, a government-chartered nonprofit organization that relies heavily on volunteers and donations.

The move surprised Labor employees and official Washington. Many assumed one of the nation's most powerful and popular women was preparing to run for office in 1992. After all, readers of a national magazine had just voted her their favorite candidate to become the nation's first female president.

To understand her resignation, however, they needed to listen to the drumbeat she had been hearing since early childhood. At times, especially as she worked long hours to build a career in public service, the beat sounded faint and uncertain. But as she moved up to positions of power and responsibility, the beat sounded loud and clear.

Library Resource Center
Renton Technical College
3000 NE 4th St.
Renton, WA 98056-4195

2

A Habit of Helping Out

Mary Elizabeth Alexander Hanford began life July 29, 1936, in the beautiful, prosperous old town of Salisbury, North Carolina. Most people knew or knew of her parents, Mary and John Van Hanford, and her thirteen-year-old brother, Johnny.

Mary Cathey Hanford had deep roots in Rowan County. Her father's family, the Catheys, was among the Scotch-Irish Presbyterians who had settled there before the American Revolution. In 1775 a Cathey had signed the Rowan Resolves calling for the thirteen colonies to unite. According to family tradition, several of her mother's ancestors, the Alexanders, had signed an even more rebellious document in neighboring Mecklenburg County.

John Hanford ran the florist business his father had started. The Hanfords had come from Illinois to the rolling hills of Rowan County in the early 1900s after reading about the area's reputation for having a healthful climate and good music in *The Land of the Sky,* a novel by a Salisbury native. Emma Hanford, John's mother, was an artist (her paintings now hang in her granddaughter's home).

Music brought Mary and John together. One day when she was practicing the organ at her church, she looked out the window to see John listening as he worked in the flower garden. He was also a musician. He played several instruments and led the town band. They chatted, and the romance between the outgoing, energetic woman and the quiet businessman began.

When the Catheys talked of taking Mary to New York to study to become a music teacher, John feared he would lose her. He asked her to give up her career plans and become his wife. She agreed. After their marriage she occasionally helped with the business but mostly devoted herself to her family and to numerous church and community activities.

When the couple had a little girl, the proud father wanted her to have her mother's name. Mary preferred her grandmother's name, Elizabeth Alexander, and refused to call the child Mary. When Elizabeth began to talk, she settled the matter by calling herself Liddy.

Liddy adored her big brother, who was an outstanding student, and wanted to be part of what he did. When she was three, he spurred her interest in elections by helping her win the honor of being the class mascot at his high school graduation. Both wore cap and gown.

The pretty child was used to receiving attention. The florist's daughter served as a flower girl at several weddings. The first time, she and another child got bored during the ceremony and began their own march back down the aisle. Their horrified mothers shooed them back to their places near the bride and groom. Her mother recalls that at later weddings Liddy, although little more than a toddler, took great care in dropping the flower petals exactly the same distance apart along her route. From the beginning, she was a perfectionist.

That didn't mean she was always perfect. Soon after the Hanfords moved into a new house on South Fulton Street, three-year-old Liddy took a private tour of her brother's room and found

The proud father, John Van Hanford, holds his six-month-old daughter, Mary Elizabeth Alexander Hanford.

thirteen comic valentines. She decorated her pink and blue bedroom by pasting these on the wall.

When her father found out what she had done, he took her to her room and asked who had put the valentines on the wall. Liddy said it had been her imaginary playmate, Denaw. Her father told her Denaw hadn't been there that day. Liddy then said Johnny had done it, but her father pointed out her big brother would have put the valentines up high. She finally admitted, "Liddy did it."

Her father then took her to each picture and asked who had put it up. As she said she had done it, he gave her a tap with a broomstraw switch. Her mother remembers that Liddy never pasted anything or colored on the walls again. Liddy remembers that disappointing her father hurt far more than the switch.

John Hanford believed in strict discipline, but he also tried to comfort his daughter when anything went wrong.

Liddy takes command of a cart pulled by a goat.

That same fateful third year, the family noticed that Liddy's eyes were crossing. Her mother had a friend take her to a specialist in Charlotte, the nearest city. Mary Hanford recalls, "He didn't say a thing about her eyes but just starting fitting her with these teeny little glasses. The tears started rolling down my face. . . . I said, 'I can just see her now wearing glasses and wearing evening dresses.'"

When they got home, John Hanford, who also wore glasses, said to the unhappy child, "This is great. You and I can have glasses. Mother and Johnny can't have glasses."

The child felt much better, "very special," her mother says. "She climbed trees, she skated, she did everything. Never did break her glasses."

Nonetheless, very few of the many pictures of Liddy in the scrapbooks her mother kept show her in the thick glasses she wore publicly until starting to use contacts in the mid-1970s. One of the early scrapbooks shows a newspaper photo of six-year-old Liddy, glassless, posing with six other children and a Girl Scout leader on the Hanfords' spiral staircase. While the mothers rolled bandages for injured soldiers as American Red Cross volunteers, the children were helping win World War II by gathering bits of such needed materials as tinfoil from chewing gun wrappers, cans, and old razor blades. Liddy took part in many such community service activities as she grew up. On their own or working through the church, the schools, and various clubs and organizations, the Hanford family made a habit of helping out.

In grade school the glasses made Liddy feel different, and they also made it hard for her to play softball. She even found reasons to stay home a day or two when she couldn't face a game. Her mother says, "She couldn't hit the ball, and she said one time, 'Mother, I'm the last one when they choose sides.' I said, 'Yes, but you're the first one when they choose sides for spelling.'"

She almost always earned gold stars in spelling. She worked hard in school and usually made excellent grades. She particularly

Here Is Salisbury's Youngest Defense Group

tle girls and a boy of pre-school age wanted
n the war. Said one little girl with starry
can knit for the soldiers." Said another:
t waste paper."

lay afternoon they all gathered at the
Elizabeth Hanford on South Fulton street
s Fannie Funderburke, itinerant Girl Scout
n duty here, offered some ideas. They
nong other things, that they could collect
re stamps and unused defense stamps, tin-

At six Liddy, second from the top, made the local newspaper with friends who helped in the war effort.

liked spelling, reading, and writing. She sometimes wrote verses, and for years she continued to do that for special occasions. In the second or third grade she wrote a poem, "The Singing Cat," about her pet:

Beauty and her kittens four
Sat on the kitchen floor.
Beauty is a singing cat,
She always loved to catch a rat.
So right now on the kitchen floor
Sits Beauty and her kittens four.

Elaine Richards, Liddy's second grade teacher, says, "She was overly conscientious and wanted to please so bad. When Liddy got her [new] glasses, her eyelashes were so long they hit the lenses. That used to worry her. She was a beautiful child."

The teacher, now retired, tells of a day Liddy forgot to bring a book to school. "I heard her kind of 'Sniff, sniff,' and I said, 'What's the matter?' She forgot her spelling or reading book—I don't remember which—for one of her assignments. I said, 'Honey, that's okay. Look at all those books over there. Just go get another one.'

" 'I want mine.' "

The teacher continues, "She just kept on, and I said 'Would it make you happy if I let you go home and get it?' "

Liddy answered, " Oh yes, oh yes, oh yes! Could I do that?"

Knowing that Liddy lived only three blocks from Wiley School, the teacher left her class of approximately forty pupils for a couple of minutes to take Liddy outside and across the street. That left her one other street to cross.

Liddy, years later, remembered feeling she was a "total failure" on that walk home.

When she arrived, Mary Hanford recalls, "She was crying her eyes out, just so upset. She said, 'I forgot my book this morning, and Mrs. Richards sent me back for it.' "

18

"Her life was ruined," her mother says, "I said, 'How great you live close enough you could run home and get your book! And what a great teacher to let you come home and get your book. I'll bet every child in there wishes they could come with you.' Before I knew it, she was all smiles and skipping back."

Elaine Richards also remembers that Liddy would sometimes bring fragrant gardenias to her from the Hanfords' greenhouses, some of which were just across the street from the school.

Liddy almost died that year. She and a friend had spent the afternoon picking out and eating hickory nuts, so when she didn't feel well that night, her mother thought little about it at first. Liddy soon grew worse, however, and the Hanfords called a doctor. He came to the house, and they wrapped Liddy in a blanket and took her to the hospital. Her appendix had burst, causing peritonitis, an infection. At that time doctors did not have antibiotics or similar medicines to fight such infections, so these often were fatal. It was several days before Liddy was out of danger. As she recovered, the hospital staff and others made a fuss over her.

Her mother prepared a new bed to welcome her home, but Mary Hanford says, "She didn't want to come home, she was having such a good time rolling [in a wheelchair] all over the hospital." The sick child received many letters and gifts, including a bride doll for her collection from Johnny, who was in the Navy. "She had dolls from all over the world," her mother says. When Liddy was a little older, she made a display of the dolls with the flags of the countries they came from for a Parent-Teacher Association meeting.

The dolls were one of her many interests. She was a busy child in a family that believed in work. Her brother says, "She was always overcommitted on her time from the time she was a little tyke." She had no chores, but she took piano lessons for ten years and ballet and tap dancing lessons for a much shorter period. She belonged to several children's organizations and freely volunteered her mother's services as cook, chauffeur, and chaperone. Many events took place at the Hanford home.

On many Saturday afternoons, Liddy and her friends would go to the movie theater next to her father's flower shop. One friend, Betty Dan Nicholas Gilliam, remembers that several of the friends' parents agreed that each child would get the same allowance. At first it was fifteen cents a week, enough to pay for the movie and a treat. As prices went up, their allowance rose to twenty-five and then fifty cents.

Betty Dan also remembers that the children teased her and Liddy about being skinny, "and skinny wasn't in. Nobody said we were nice and thin."

In the third grade, imitating her mother's activities, Liddy organized the Bird Club. The members elected her president. A scrapbook shows that Elizabeth Hanford set up—even though she couldn't spell them—five "committies," social, plant and flower, special program, clean-up, and health.

Liddy rarely got into trouble, but her mother remembers, "A little boy in her room in school came to play, and they found some cigarettes in John's room. The boy's mother called me when he went home and said he had singed his eyelashes. We really worked on her about that."

Former Wiley School principal Harold Isenberg says that he had only good reports about Liddy. In fact most of the children were well-behaved. In those days, if they weren't, educators sometimes used what they called the "board of education"—a paddle. Salisbury was known for its good schools. Like most of the country at that time, the town had a two-part system—one for whites and one for African Americans.

Liddy's family lived in a lovely three-story Tudor home on a street with fine houses, and, Isenberg says, she "could have been less than democratic in her reactions to other children." Instead, he says, "Liddy's friends were the students in her class, and it made no difference where they lived or what their parents did."

The children all walked to school and ate the lunches they brought there. He says the teachers told him Liddy was exchanging her nice lunches with poor children, especially one girl, whose sandwiches would have nothing between the bread but a piece of bologna or a bit of margarine. When a child would ask Liddy what she had that day, Liddy would say, "I'm not certain. Would you like to trade with me?" In this way Liddy not only gave her friend a good lunch but also made her feel she was not receiving charity.

3

A Good Start

After working in Washington, D.C., under six presidents, Elizabeth Hanford Dole still calls her hometown "my personal Rock of Gibraltar."

For Liddy and her friends, Salisbury was a good place to grow up. Residents were proud of the part the town played in the American Revolution, and Liddy was active in the Children of the American Revolution, the junior branch of the Daughters of the American Revolution. Her mother and friends' mothers worked to preserve the town's fine old buildings and historic atmosphere.

Religion always has been a strong force in the town. One of the main streets is Church Street, and several large churches make the name appropriate even today. The churches sponsored numerous activities for the children, including Boy and Girl Scouts and youth groups. Liddy took part in many church activities, and on Sunday afternoons she went to her grandmother's home to listen to Bible stories.

Church and school youth groups often met at the Hanford family's cabin, a small house on a farm near Salisbury. Such features as a pool made by damming up a stream, a cool pine grove, and a dishwasher for easy clean-ups made it especially popular during the warm summers.

Throughout most of its history, the town has had a healthy economy. The most notable exception was during and after the Civil War. During the war, the town was the site of a large prison camp for Union soldiers. Memorials to the thousands who died there dot the National Cemetery, and a few blocks away, on Church Street, a large statue honors Rowan County's Confederate soldiers. Salisbury long has been a county seat and transportation hub, with roads and then railroads taking goods in and out. The county has been agricultural, with farmers raising a variety of crops. Small businesses, textile mills, and other industries have provided employment.

Liddy was born during the heart of the Depression. Many people lost jobs and businesses, but people continued to buy flowers for special occasions. Her father expanded his business to sell flowers not just to townspeople but to other florists around the South. He grew plants in giant greenhouses on the family's farm, and after World War II he imported plants from other countries. Liddy had little to do with the business, but she remembers the excitement when the first plane landed with flowers from abroad.

Salisbury's economic and cultural life benefited from the presence of two respected colleges, Livingstone, founded in 1879 to educate black men and women, and Catawba, a church-related college that relocated there before Liddy was born. The colleges offered many concerts, plays, art exhibits, and other cultural events uncommon in a town of 20,000 to 25,000 people.

World War II brought some hardships, such as the rationing of food, gasoline, and many other items, and Liddy's adored big brother was one of those who went off to fight the war. Liddy and her friends had no television, but they saw what was happening in the war in the short news films shown before the main feature at the movie theater.

After the war another great threat hung over the children's heads for several summers. That was polio, an infectious disease that killed or crippled most who caught it. To prevent the spread of the disease during its worst periods, the country club closed its swimming pool, and children were not allowed to go to the movies or to restaurants.

Liddy often went to camp in the mountains or to the beach in the summers. One return from the beach was a very sad one. The Hanfords had two chihuahuas, and Liddy doted on one named Penny. She asked her parents to bring the little dog when they came to the beach to pick up her and a friend. While the Hanfords were at their cabin, however, the dog apparently ate some poison a neighboring farmer had put out for pests. Liddy's father and brother rushed Penny to a veterinarian, but the pet died.

Liddy had always loved animals. Once, when she was small, her grandmother had even found her hiding a bug under the hall carpet so her mother wouldn't see it and kill it. The Hanfords knew the dog's death would upset her, so they phoned to tell her to return by bus. When the dog didn't greet her, Liddy said, "Penny's dead, isn't she?" She burst into tears, as she would do many more times. She would hold the other chihuahua, Pepi, and it would lick the tears from her cheeks.

When Liddy won a fire prevention essay contest, she used the prize money to have a photograph of Penny made into a stand-up cutout as a gift for her father. The cutout still stands on a shelf in the Hanford home among Liddy's awards and photos. The fire department still has the essay.

Liddy also won a prize and a few dollars for a paper on her sixth grade teacher that she sent to a contest run by a popular network radio show, "The Quiz Kids."

That teacher, like several others, took special interest in Liddy and other students' progress. One night she came to the Hanfords

Penny, a chihuahua that died tragically, was one of Liddy's most loved pets.

to talk about Liddy's handwriting being different on each paper. She wanted Liddy to choose one way to write and use only that.

Mary Hanford says, "So we got out some of John's writing and some of my writing. My daughter tried several, and we decided which we liked the best. From then on she stuck to that." The handwriting selected has large, rounded letters.

An avid reader, Liddy decided to start a book club like her mother's for her friends. Liddy invited several to join her Junior Book Club and named herself president. The group met in homes and had speakers and refreshments. One meeting featured a talk by a woman who had been in Japan, a country Liddy determined to visit. She already loved to travel. Her family took a vacation trip most summers, but they rarely went farther than Canada or the West.

At the end of the sixth grade, Liddy's teacher wrote a letter to the Hanfords saying, "Elizabeth stood right among the toppers in the achievement test recently, but the thing that gives me most joy is the quality of her daily work. Nothing is ever too unimportant to do well, which is quite a good character trait to possess, I think. And Elizabeth now knows how to take notes, express herself in the written and spoken word, do research work, travel and get the benefits thereof, which are quite accomplishments for a sixth grader. What's more, she is seven months ahead in arithmetic achievement. Figuring is not a bugbear to her any more, so far as I can see. Such pupils are the reason teaching is always a joy."

Coming from a musical family, Liddy took ten years of piano lessons. She says, "I remember my dad didn't want to sit through long [recital] concerts. He would figure out when I was coming on, and then he would go outside and smoke his cigar all through the pieces up to that point. He would be in his chair when his daughter came out."

During the seventh or eighth grade Liddy and three or four other good friends, some of whom attended other schools, formed the Debs, a nickname for debutantes. One Deb, Jean Stanback Brumley, says it was "a group of friends who were going to band together and do some things." They helped each other plan and carry out church and school activities. After they all entered Boyden High School in ninth grade, the group grew to include eighteen girls.

Eighth grade graduation was an important event for students in Salisbury. As Liddy was well aware, Johnny had received the citizenship cup when he graduated. Mary Hanford remembers Liddy coming to her before they went to the graduation ceremony and saying, "I have tried my best to do real good work, but I don't think I'm going to get anything. I don't want you to be disappointed."

Her mother answered, "Oh, heavens! We don't have to get the cup. You've done so well, and you've had such a good time, and you've gained so much this year. The cup wouldn't matter. Let's forget about the cup."

That night Liddy received two cups, one for citizenship and one for an essay she had written after doing much research.

The high school years were even busier. As usual, Liddy worked hard and made top grades. For her, one of the most frustrating classes was home economics. Conjugating Latin verbs proved easier than putting in a zipper.

She took part in many extracurricular activities, including student government, the drama club, the newspaper, and the National Honor Society. She also led an active social life. Students tended to go out in groups or on double dates, and the girls, especially the Debs, sometimes had slumber parties after a dance or ball game.

Homecoming was a major event, and students spent many hours constructing floats for the parade. Jean Brumley remembers building a huge chicken out of chicken wire and napkins atop her brother's red convertible in the Hanfords' back yard. The sign said, "We're laying for" the opposing team.

Every year students raised money for school activities by selling magazine subscriptions. They competed fiercely to sell the most, with the top sellers receiving prizes. Liddy usually placed high. She had a special sales technique. She talked grandmothers into buying subscriptions as Christmas gifts for their grandchildren. One year she won a radio that still sits in the Hanford breakfast room.

The girls wore gored skirts or full poodle skirts with crinoline petticoats. They went to sock hops, informal dances named after the bobby socks they wore, sometimes with a liner sock inside and the two rolled down around the ankle. For formal dances, such as the all-important junior-senior prom, the girls wanted strapless gowns with a bit of fluff around the top and ruffles all the way down.

Girls didn't wear jeans or slacks to school or on dates. In the summer they would wear pedal pushers, which were slacks ending midway between the ankle and the knee, or bermudas, which were shorts that came almost to the knee.

Betty Dan Nicholas Gilliam, one of the Debs, says, "Angora sweaters were a must in every girl's wardrobe. We even put them in the refrigerator so they would fluff out."

As a high school senior, Liddy campaigned unsuccessfully for school president.

Betty Dan remembers that Liddy seemed rather glamorous to the other girls. She was always well dressed, and she made her glasses stylish by painting the frames to match her outfits with her brother's model airplane paint. When the mother of one of the founding Debs, Wyndham Robertson, returned from a trip to New York with word of frames with rhinestones, Liddy got a pair for dressy occasions.

Fashion was important for the young ladies, as the teenagers were called. Betty Dan says, "We wore hats and gloves to church, luncheons, and grown-up teas."

Almost none of the girls the Debs knew—and few boys—did anything as scandalous as drinking beer in high school. "Nobody was smoking openly," Betty Dan says. "Kids tried cigarettes, maybe at a slumber party. No one was carrying them around."

Adults chaperoned all events, and the mothers got together to decide what time their daughters had to be in and where they could go on dates. Liddy and her friends rarely got in trouble for anything more serious than being a few minutes late, perhaps because, as her mother says, "They had mamas who were right behind them." That was literally true when the teenagers went on hayrides. Mothers would drive behind the wagon with the car lights shining on their offspring.

In Liddy's senior year, she ran for school president. This was considered a boy's job, but she had been president of the Senior Methodist Youth Fellowship, the Rowan Resolves Society of the Children of the American Revolution, and her class. She and her supporters made signs and banners and ran ads for the slate in the school newspaper. They made handouts consisting of a piece of red paper with a little wooden spoon attached and the slogan, "Stir yourself a vote for Liddy Hanford."

When some boys tore down her campaign signs, her mother says, "It didn't seem to bother her. She felt real complimented." She saw the destruction as a sign the boys were taking her candidacy seriously.

In a campaign speech, Liddy said, "More and more the modern world is giving women a big part to play. Women must keep pace in the world."

In spite of Liddy and her friends' hard work and her obvious qualifications, she lost the election. It was a big disappointment. Jean Brumley says, "Losses taught her running well and losing well." Liddy also learned to focus on her goals and to prepare well.

4

Try, Try Again

Liddy had many successes her senior year. She received both state and national citations for her work as the local and state junior chairman of the Children of the American Revolution radio and television committee. She was elected secretary for the western district of the North Carolina Student Council Congress. Her classmates voted her the girl "most likely to succeed."

One of her male classmates recalls joking that Liddy would be the first "lady president." Betty Dan says, "Since we were little kids, we have never doubted that Liddy would be president of the United States. She has always been a leader."

A school publication with a write-up on each of the 144 graduating seniors entitled hers "Likeable Liddy." In tribute to her participation in French Club and the traveling she had done with her parents, it suggested her secret ambition was to become a French interpreter in an airport. It also made note of the young Marine she was dating, saying, "Don't be surprised if you hear strains of the Marine Hymn coming from the Hanford home. It happens to be her favorite song."

Although the Marine earned a prominent place in her high school scrapbook, the romance never became serious.

Liddy and the young man voted "most likely to succeed" pose for a picture for a high school publication in 1954.

At one of the last of the high school parties, everyone came as a "suppressed ambition." Liddy came as a traveler. Although she had been interested in student government since third grade, she had not yet thought of government as a career. Her ambitions changed from time to time. She says, "I remember at one point thinking of Christian education."

Jean doesn't remember Liddy considering a political, or any other, career while in high school. Jean says, "There wasn't as much focus on careers in high school then as there is today. The general expectation for girls at that stage was still to get married when you finished college." Raising a family became the woman's career, along with volunteer work and participation in community and social activities.

Although Liddy's family discussed political affairs, they were not directly involved in politics. Her grandfather, Joseph Pinkney Cathey, voted Democratic no matter who was running. Her father registered as a Democrat only so he could vote in that party's primaries (a win in the Democratic primary virtually assured a win in the general election in those years in North Carolina), and he gave the Republicans a place for their headquarters in a downtown building. When General Dwight Eisenhower ran for president as a Republican in 1952, John Hanford—like thousands of other Southern Democrats—registered as a Republican.

What the girls worried about in their senior year was where to go to college. Many of the Debs applied to women's colleges. Liddy and Jean wanted to go to Duke University in Durham. Her brother, John, who had become a partner in the floral company, had built an outstanding record there. Liddy didn't even apply anywhere else. Her excellent grades and many extracurricular activities earned her admission, and that spring she became one of fifteen finalists for three Angier Duke scholarships. She went to the university for interviews and felt encouraged when one of the interviewers told her she had done well. Her mother thought the remark meant she hadn't won a scholarship. That night Liddy asked her brother what he thought, and he agreed with their mother. Tears began to roll down Liddy's cheeks.

John made a joke of it. "Why are you crying? Dad's the one who should be crying. He's the one who's got to pay for four years of college."

She laughed, and the tears stopped. Liddy rarely was down for long. When she was, she tried not to show it.

At the high school graduation ceremony, Liddy was one of five students selected to give a valedictory speech. Hers began, "In this age of vastly increased tensions, this confused, complex age, we often need to look to someone for reassurance, encouragement, and inspiration. The lives of great men all remind us of their difficulties, sorrows, and disappointments." She went on to discuss the achievements of George Washington, Thomas Jefferson, and other presidents.

When Liddy left for college, her mother said to her, "Let's leave 'Liddy' at home," but the nickname went with her.

In 1954 Duke University had separate campuses for men and women. Approximately 1,200 women lived and attended almost all their classes on the older East Campus. More than a mile away, approximately 2,300 men lived and went to almost all their classes on the West Campus. A student took a class on the other campus only when it was not available on the student's own campus. Each campus had its own student government, but the male majority dominated campus life.

Liddy and Jean, who had met when they were only a few days old, took rooms in different dormitories so they would meet new people. Liddy soon decided to major in political science and international affairs. Her mother had hoped the bright girl would major in home economics, marry, and live in Salisbury, preferably just down the street. Worried, Mary Hanford talked to a Duke professor about the strange major.

"Let her take political science," the professor said. "We need women in government. And anyway, they all get married eventually."

Looking back, the successful woman says, "Although I didn't have a blueprint of where I wanted to go or what I wanted to do, it was just a natural love of government, of working with people, of selling an idea. I love that part of trying to convince people of an idea.

"I used to think that I would make a good salesperson because I like to get in there and talk about what I believe in. It was a natural thing to major in political science and run for student offices. That led to Washington eventually."

The freshman year is the most difficult one for most students, and as a new Duchess, as women students at Duke were called, Liddy faced both trials and triumphs. A major disappointment was losing the election to student government. Not one to give up, she joined in various other campus activities and tried again the next year. This time she won.

Near the end of her freshman year, she and four other Debs received invitations to take part in an annual spring debutante cotillion at Raleigh. The organizers staged the ball for approximately fifty select young women from eastern North Carolina towns too small to put on their own cotillions. The event served as the traditional coming-out ball, which originally was given to introduce marriageable young ladies to eligible gentlemen. Jean says, "It was really a bit of an honor for the girls' families—and wonderfully fun for the girls."

Each father presented his daughter, who wore a white evening dress and carried roses. Each girl had, as Jean remembers, a brother or boyfriend as marshall and two other young men to be part of the stag line. That assured that every debutante had plenty of chances to dance. The spring cotillion was just the beginning. Throughout the spring and summer the young women, singly or in small groups,

While a freshman at Duke University, Liddy attended a regional debutante ball in Raleigh.

gave cotillions to which they invited all the others. The Salisbury friends cosponsored one.

Although Liddy enjoyed such social events, she didn't let them interfere with her school work. By her junior and senior years she had begun to make choices and set priorities in her activities, concentrating her efforts on student government and the college yearbook. Even so, she had an extremely heavy schedule. Jean recalls, "She always was kind of a last-minute person. She could pack more into a time frame!" Liddy sometimes would go home for the weekend to complete a major assignment without interruptions. She would do the same while in law school—and while preparing to become president of the American Red Cross.

More than thirty years later she says, "I think there is no substitute for establishing good work and study habits because they will serve you a lifetime. I always felt you need to really isolate yourself. To be in a group setting where you are constantly talking back and forth or to have loud music or whatever, that doesn't work for me. I just figure, 'All right, I'm going to get it done so I can go and enjoy visiting with friends.' "

She applies those study habits to her working habits today. She says, "In preparing a speech, for example, I like to sit down and outline and think, 'Now what are the major points I want to get across here?'

"Or if you are going to be interviewed on television and it's going to be quick and you can't expound, you need to go in with three or four or five things on that subject that you feel are really important and know how to work those in to the questions that are asked."

Both toasted and criticized in Washington for the thoroughness of her preparation, she says, "Mother used to say, 'If it's worth doing, it's worth giving it your best.' It's just a matter of living up to your own standards. Not so much of competing against others as of meeting the standards you set for yourself."

She continues, "That has a lot to do with the diligence I put into my efforts. That's just the way I do things. I'm not comfortable with a lick and a prayer. I think if you realize there's a point of diminishing returns, this works well. Because if you are conscientious, you're going to be prepared, you're going to do your best, you're going to give your best presentation, and that's going to be an asset rather than a liability."

Near the end of her junior year, Liddy ran for president of the Women's Student Government Association (WSGA) and won. Shortly after her election, two editorials in the school newspaper criticized the new president. One, entitled "Top Secrets," concerned a lack of open action on a student honor code. It read, in part, "The newly-elected officers promised in their pre-election addresses to keep the women informed of what the Council was doing; many coeds voted for them because of this growing need on East to know of and think about student government without having previously-made decisions handed down on a silver platter. A complete reversal of this election promise is the refusal of the WSGA president to make known the progress of work on the Honor Code."

The editorial ended by calling for "the leadership of WSGA to promote intelligent discussions and decisions by the entire campus. Needless secrecy will provide neither leadership nor success."

Another criticized Liddy's manner of conducting a meeting, saying, "The 'Call to Order' began the WSGA meeting Monday night, and that was the first and last order we had at the final assembly of the year." The first few minutes were quiet except for "the clacking of knitting needles and flipping of textbook pages," the editorial said, "But new business brought such chaos as has not been seen all year."

Although years later she dismisses the comments on her parliamentary abilities as "just the normal healthy tensions between the government and the press," the words had hurt.

Liddy responded to the criticisms by taking several corrective measures. She convinced the dean to permit the new officers to hold a planning retreat at the Hanfords' cabin and the beach. At a time when Duke required female students to sign out of the dormitories in the evening and to be in by 10:30 on school nights, the retreat made the front page of the college newspaper.

Liddy spent much of her summer vacation taking classes at the University of Colorado in order to lighten the academic load her senior year and have more time for student government. She also spent many hours studying *Robert's Rules of Order,* the basic book of parliamentary procedure. Never again would anyone accuse her of not knowing how to conduct a meeting.

5

The Roundabout Route to Law School

In Colorado Liddy discovered she could be a good athlete, something her misadventures playing softball and her frustrations in her college golf class had made her doubt. Some expert instruction and practice turned her into a competent, confident waterskier.

She had been dating a young man in Salisbury who waterskied. Usually he and a male friend skied while Liddy and another young woman ran the boat for them. When she got back from Colorado, the young man invited her to go out for some waterskiing, and she gladly agreed.

On the way to the water, the men said that they had been having trouble with the boat and might not be able to ski much, so when they asked who wanted to ski first, Liddy surprised them by saying that she did. Her mother says, "She couldn't wait to show them, to show off. . . . She still enjoys [waterskiing]." Part of the pleasure apparently came from the chance to match her date's skills when the tendency was, as her mother says, for the boys to "sort of push the girls aside."

Back at Duke, Liddy faced a major controversy over a proposed honor code that would obligate students not to cheat and to report those who did. Violators would go before an Honor Council for a kind of trial. After lively debate on both campuses that fall, the students voted in late November. The women, the East Campus, voted for the code 666 to 363, with very few students not voting. Fewer than half the men, the West Campus, voted, with 463 favoring it and 453 opposing it. Although a majority of those voting had favored the honor code, fewer than half the students had approved it, so it didn't pass.

The school newspaper praised WSGA, and thereby Liddy, in an editorial, saying, "Although the newly-deceased honor code campaign was a magnificent failure, the Women's Student Government Association can afford a bit of back-patting for the outstanding job it did in presenting the code. The campaign was exemplary of the fine administration which is the rule with WSGA." It went on to say the campaign had been "marked by unity," a "determined and unchanging stand," "a noteworthy lack of high pressure salesmanship," and "quiet efficiency."

Liddy didn't let the matter end there. She and three other student leaders, including two from the West Campus, began to work quietly on a limited honor code that would require the unanimous approval of each class and that would affect only certain courses. They presented the compromise to the undergraduate faculty council in the spring.

Meantime she had been working on other issues, including giving women students the right to be on campus (but not in class) in their bermuda shorts.

The student government experience, and particularly getting a part of a measure approved when the whole could not be passed, gave Liddy some vital lessons in governing.

Today she says, "What I found to be so useful there was that you had the opportunity to mediate between the needs of the faculty, the students, the administration and the trustees—that mediation role meant a lot to me—as well as having to stand on your two feet and express yourself, to articulate your views on what you cared about and drive your goals home. All of that, to me, is excellent practice for the real world. I really am a strong believer in student government. That was a learning experience that was invaluable to me."

Jean also sees her old friend's student government experience as important and says, "She's a good mediator. She doesn't threaten people in the process of trying to negotiate and make things better, which, I think, is probably one of the keys to her success."

Student government was not her only activity her senior year. She was also business manager of the yearbook, secretary of Delta Delta Delta sorority, and a member of the White Duchy, an honorary society that took in only seven women each year. She also made Phi Beta Kappa, the national scholastic honorary society for top students.

As the senior year ended, the women's campus elected Liddy May Queen, and she reigned over a semiformal dance in which the band played on a carousel in the middle of the dance floor.

More important, Duke named her the 1958 Leader of the Year—for both campuses. The school newspaper's editorial, written by the same student who had criticized her a year before, began, "Through Miss Hanford's direction and imagination the entire University, not just East Campus or WSGA, has been left with many long-term improvements."

The editor continued, "WSGA itself was perhaps the pinnacle of campus organizations this year because of Miss Hanford's leadership. The leadership training program, the Foreign Student Committee, the excellent relations with the Administration, the nearly 100 other specific accomplishments provided unequalled service to the campus."

It had been a hectic, triumphant senior year, but what came next? Liddy was "pinned" to a young man attending another college, but she wasn't ready to get married, as Jean did. Liddy's family wanted her to enter the family business. Knowing she liked to write and to travel, her brother tried to tempt her with the chance to write a newsletter or to travel to other countries as a buyer.

Among the attractions of Salisbury were her young nephews, John and Jody. Often when Liddy came home from Duke on weekends or holidays, John stayed at his grandparents' home. If Liddy slept late, the toddler enjoyed waking her to come to breakfast. His grandmother would pull the sheet out from the foot of the bed, and John would tickle Liddy's feet.

Liddy looked for an interesting job near her hometown, including at the newspaper in Charlotte. There she found that an outstanding student record and winning essays weren't enough to get a job. Ironically, in 1986 the paper invited her to speak at its centennial celebration. In the audience was a South Carolina newspaper editor, the man who had written the editorials criticizing her conduct of the meeting and praising her for her accomplishments as East Campus president. He told her he remembered only the latter.

Although her parents would have liked for her to stay in Salisbury and marry, she decided to leave. She says, "They never pushed me to conform to a mold, no matter what they might have thought or what they might have liked."

Liddy wanted to do graduate work in another part of the country. She says, "I was thinking that law might be a very good background for a career in government service. That was beginning to jell, but it wasn't yet a plan or a blueprint.

"For young people, women and men, I do recommend that they map out what they want to do and plan it out," she says, "but I don't think many of my generation did that."

The choice narrowed to New York and Boston. She had friends in both places. Her family favored Boston's academic environment. Liddy went there and stayed with friends while hunting for a job at Harvard University, which is just outside Boston in Cambridge. The high achiever took a traditional woman's job, secretary to the head librarian of Harvard Law School Library.

She hadn't studied shorthand, and she had learned to type in a summer course in early high school. She remembers, "I started out as many other secretaries do, going back at night trying to retype all the things that I hadn't gotten quite right during the day."

She doesn't regret the decision. "All of us start with something that's not our ideal, but you get your foot in the door and you prove yourself and go on from there into things that will be much more meaningful." She believes the job helped lead her into law school.

Liddy liked the north. That winter she found she loved to ski on snow as well as on water.

The next summer, 1959, she went to England's Oxford University to study English history and government. She explored Oxford and its surroundings on a bicycle and spent weekends traveling to other parts of the United Kingdom. She also began dating a North Carolinian she had met at Duke and who was studying medicine at Harvard.

When she got a chance to visit the Soviet Union, she filled a sheet with arguments on why she should go and called her parents to convince them. Her father regarded the Soviet Union as such a dangerous enemy that he had built a bomb shelter, but she persuaded him this would be another "enriching experience," a phrase she used often in those days.

While in the Soviet Union she experienced a bit of the tension of life in a police state when she persuaded a young man to take her with him to visit his mother. The woman welcomed her but kept the radio turned up so they could not be overheard.

That fall Liddy enrolled in a master of arts in teaching program at Harvard with a joint major in government. The teaching degree was "a vocational insurance policy." At that time, educated women had three major job opportunities—teaching, nursing, and secretarial work.

She enjoyed her student teaching assignment, an eleventh grade history class at a suburban school. Her supervisor told her she was a born teacher, but Liddy was still thinking about law school and government, not teaching.

The next summer, 1960, she headed for Washington, D.C., and found a secretarial job in the office of Senator B. Everett Jordan, a North Carolina Democrat. Suzanne Rodgers Bush, a staff member and Liddy's summer housemate, says, "She was vivacious and very outgoing and attractive. She just seemed to have everything going for her. She was very interested in getting involved in politics. She wasn't very well defined in what she believed in." Suzanne notes a rare trait, saying, "She had malice toward none."

Senator Jordan released Suzanne to help with the Democrats' Southern campaign. Liddy, with her customary thirst for a new experience, volunteered to help out. They worked as greeters on a whistle-stop tour, a campaign conducted from a train, with the candidate for vice-president, Lyndon B. Johnson. He was running with John F. Kennedy, who became the nation's first Catholic president.

Suzanne also remembers, "She dated interesting young men," often young men with promising political futures. "We kidded her and said, 'You are either going to marry somebody going to the White House or you are going to get there yourself.' She was very oriented to politics."

Liddy constantly consulted with friends and her mother, via the telephone, about boyfriends and various other things. Suzanne says, "She has always been the kind of person to seek advice."

She sought out professional women to get their advice on pursuing a career in government. The most famous of these was Senator Margaret Chase Smith, a Republican from Maine who had been appointed to complete her husband's term upon his death and then captured and held the office on her own. The senator advised the young woman to go to law school.

Liddy returned to her job in the law library for two more years. In the summers of 1961 and 1962 she worked at the United Nations in New York. She had been told that the United Nations didn't hire anyone just for the summer or who didn't speak five languages, but she decided to check it out for herself. That particular summer the U.N. needed additional guides, so she got the job, and an important insight into job hunting—it never hurts to try.

In the spring of 1962 she applied to Harvard Law School. That summer she and the medical student she had been dating broke up. Later she indicated that he couldn't understand her great enthusiasm for the "global village," "common man," and politics, and she couldn't accept his lack of enthusiasm for these subjects.

When the law school accepted her, she broke the news to her family. No one was overjoyed. Her brother asked, "Do you really want to bury yourself in a monastery for three years?" Her mother feared she was giving up any possibility of becoming a wife and mother. Liddy assured them she would try it for a year before deciding whether to complete the three-year program.

That fall, at age twenty-six, she became one of two dozen women in a Harvard Law School class of 550. One of the women a year ahead of her was Patricia Schroeder, now a representative from Colorado. One of those a year behind was Judith W. Rogers, the D.C. Court of Appeals chief judge who gave the oath of office to Elizabeth Hanford Dole for the position of secretary of labor.

At last Liddy began to be called Elizabeth, although all her old Salisbury friends and many dating from later days still call her Liddy.

On her first day of class, one of the men came up to her and asked what she was doing there. "Don't you realize," he scolded, "there are men who would give their right arm to be in the law school—men who would *use* their legal education?"

She tells this story frequently, but she never names the man, who is now a partner in a Washington, D.C., law firm. She says,

46

"You'd be amazed at the number of my male classmates who've called me to say, 'Elizabeth, please tell me I'm not the one.' "

It was a difficult year, with at least one professor decidedly unenthusiastic about women students. The volume of work was huge, and the competition was so fierce some students tore pages out of textbooks to keep other students from reading the material.

Her parents didn't know until the last minute whether she would return to Harvard for the second year, but Elizabeth went back for more. She was particularly interested in international law, and the international law club elected her president. Before she graduated in 1965, the class elected her secretary, a lifetime position.

Elizabeth lines up with members of Harvard's international law club, of which she was president.

6

Capital Time

As Elizabeth was completing her degree at one of the nation's top law schools, she had to decide what route her career would take. Her family opposed her going to New York, which is the nation's corporate legal center. Besides, she had entered law school with the idea of getting a good background for public service. Washington, D.C., a day's drive or short flight from home, was, she says "a magnet."

Elizabeth learned of a new White House Fellows program that was offering fifteen apprenticeships to the brightest and best young Americans interested in working for the federal government. She, and 3,000 others, applied. After months of writing essays and facing interviewers, Elizabeth made it to the finals with two other women and forty-two men.

The judges and the forty-five finalists met at a retreat near the capital for the last round of interviews. With her usual drive for perfection, Elizabeth turned away from the temptation of the swimming pool for another cram session in her room. She thinks this decision may have cost her the fellowship. As she learned after her interview, one of the judges passed by the pool and hinted that they were looking for people who would go back to their home states to use their Washington experience in their communities. Elizabeth feels she would have done well during the interview to admit that she was considering returning to North Carolina to run for office some day. Instead she spoke only of working in Washington.

Talking about her disappointment, Elizabeth said, "You learn from your losses. Anything that disappoints brings strength from adversity. Adversity builds your backbone."

Elizabeth took a few months off to travel before starting her career. She recalls, "My mother and a friend of hers were interested in doing something I wanted to do, which was to drive across country. I thought, 'Here's the time. I'll never have another chance.' I was curious to see how the country changes all the way across."

Without telling her mother, Elizabeth took along her passport in the hope of going on to the Orient. In San Francisco her mother said Elizabeth could continue without her if she could find "a friend, another girl, who would really like to do this, but not alone."

Elizabeth found a friend of a friend to go along. While preparing to leave, she had several interviews with major law firms. She says, "I think that's when I became absolutely convinced this is not really right, not my cup of tea. It's public service work."

The young women visited several countries, including Japan. Elizabeth remembers, "I was just fascinated with the culture, whether it was the flower arranging or the tea ceremony. It was such a different world." She would later visit Japan again on official business.

After the long holiday, Elizabeth moved to Washington, sharing an eighteenth-century house in Georgetown with three single women as newcomers commonly did. Japanese dinners became her specialty for entertaining friends. She studied for the bar examination that would give her the right to practice law and passed it in early 1966.

Elizabeth came to the capital at a time of change. Under

President John F. Kennedy's New Frontier and, following his assassination in 1963, President Lyndon B. Johnson's Great Society, the federal government had launched a series of antipoverty programs. These included Head Start for disadvantaged preschoolers and the Job Corps for unemployed young adults.

Martin Luther King, Jr., and others were leading civil rights marches. Students and others were demonstrating against American involvement in Vietnam. Women were raising the public's consciousness about the unequal treatment they were receiving in education, work, the home, and other places.

Making the rounds of government employment offices in early 1966, Elizabeth found a managerial-level entry point into government service at the Department of Health, Education, and Welfare (HEW). The position drew on the planning, organizing, and interpersonal skills she had been developing since she organized the Bird Club with five committees in third grade.

Her assignment was to organize a national conference for the newly created National Advisory Committee on Education of the Deaf and to oversee the publishing of its report. Committee members were a dozen experts, most of them educators, from all over the country.

As conference coordinator, Elizabeth chaired the committee's planning meetings. Charlotte Coffield, then an interpreter for the deaf and a secretary, says that Elizabeth ran the meetings very well. Often those attending knew each other by reputation but not by face, so Elizabeth made up a seating chart. To identify a speaker, the listeners could glance down at the chart.

Coffield says, "She was very thorough and very precise about what she was doing. She seemed to have been a very dedicated person. She dealt with people in a very smooth and gracious manner. She had a way of making people very comfortable in her presence."

Coffield didn't attend the conference in Colorado in April 1967, but she heard good things about Elizabeth's work there, which included adjusting the schedule around an unexpected blizzard. Coffield says, "If they wanted things done or things to happen, they could approach her. She was flexible, and she could handle things and smooth them out in an easy way—a very tactful person."

Coffield recalls her first impressions of the young Southerner, saying, "She sort of stood out. She was the kind of person you would look at twice. It was the way she carried herself and also the way she conducted herself. She was always a lady."

One small incident made a deep impression on the young African-American secretary, who stayed with HEW (later the Department of Education) to become a program specialist in the Deafness and Communicative Disorders Branch. Elizabeth and some other women in the office were planning a short vacation in the Virgin Islands, and Elizabeth invited Charlotte to join them. "And she meant it," says Charlotte. "Not everyone would have done that."

When the job ended, Elizabeth decided to devote a couple of months to learning the workings of criminal court so she would be qualified to defend those who could not afford to hire lawyers. She had not had trial experience during law school, so with her usual zeal for proper preparation, she went to night court to observe and learn. On the third night, the judge called the pretty, innocent-faced young Southerner to the bench and asked who she was and if she was a member of the bar. Then, despite her initial protests, he ordered her to take a case.

Her client was a Greek citizen and former zookeeper who had been arrested for annoying a lion at the National Zoo by petting the beast. Elizabeth went into the holding area, where those behind the bars gave catcalls and made remarks about the "lady lawyer." Her client spoke little English, but he did manage to say he planned to go to New York and never come back to Washington. The judge

51

gave her no time to prepare her case, and on her way to the courtroom a group of strangers asked her what she was going to do.

"It's ridiculous to keep a man locked up on a charge like annoying and petting a lion in the zoo," she told them. "If I get him out, he's not coming back. So we're going to trial tonight, even though I've never seen a trial except on Perry Mason." She then realized that she was talking to reporters and that her first appearance as a lawyer had become entertainment for the press.

When she took her place, she saw that the prosecuting attorney was a former law school classmate—the number one student in her class. Elizabeth argued that her client should go free, for without the lion there as a witness, it was impossible to know whether it had been annoyed or teased by the petting. The prosecutor asked the judge to hold her client because he not only had petted the lion but also had climbed, some weeks before, into an antelope pen.

The judge asked the defendant's word that he would not return to the zoo and when, with Elizabeth's coaching, he made the promise, let him go. She had won her first case.

The judge warned her that if she practiced in his court, she would see things she had never imagined in her sheltered world, and he sent her down to the cell block to see a man going through the agony of drug withdrawal.

The sight disturbed her, but it didn't stop her. For more than a year she worked as a public defender and received a kind of education not available in her small Southern hometown or at Harvard. She says, "The two months just expanded. I got caught up in it. It was fascinating. It was such a way to open your eyes to the problems of the inner city. I was fearless, as young people are. I would go pick up witnesses and ride them around in my car and drive into areas at night you really shouldn't, a woman alone, to pick up somebody."

At the same time she worked as a public defender, she was job hunting. She decided to accept the invitation of one of the White

House Fellows' judges, the head of the Civil Service Commission, to come see him. From his staff she heard about a fascinating job in a White House office dealing with consumer issues. When she went to be interviewed, she found the only problem was that the budget didn't cover the position. As was the case with many White House positions, an agency would have to provide the position slot.

Elizabeth went to see the head of the Food and Drug Administration, whom she had met while at HEW. He had suggested then that she should consider working with consumer affairs. He agreed to put her on the FDA payroll and transfer the slot to the White House.

She began work there in April 1968, a few months before her thirty-second birthday. After some useful meanderings, she had found her route to a career in public service.

Consumerism was one of the movements to establish individuals' rights to fair treatment in the marketplace. Consumer activists attacked such problems as deceptive advertising, inferior and dangerous products, and companies' refusals to take responsibility for broken or harmful products. Working with the movement gave Elizabeth the opportunity to deal with issues affecting millions of people's daily lives.

Her title was deputy assistant for legislative affairs, which meant she helped try to convince Congress to approve the Johnson administration's consumer policies.

Weighed down by the Vietnam war, Johnson decided not to run again. In January 1969 the Democrats moved out of the White House offices, and the Republicans, led by President Richard M. Nixon, moved in. Elizabeth's future was uncertain. She was a civil servant rather than a political appointee, but she had been part of the Johnson administration. Also, President Nixon had not been a strong consumer advocate, and he could abolish the office. Instead he renamed it the President's Committee on Consumer Interests and appointed as director Virginia Knauer, a Pennsylvania Republican who had headed that state's consumer protection office.

Knauer kept most of the staff and very soon gave Elizabeth a big promotion. Knauer told reporters Elizabeth was "a tremendously dedicated worker," "very beautiful, always a lady," and gave "exquisite parties." Using a favorite phrase from consumer protection in announcing the promotion, Knauer said, "In this very deceptive package is a Harvard-trained brain."

The new director and her young assistant worked well together, and they formed both a close personal and professional relationship. (A decade later, Virginia Knauer would work for Elizabeth in another White House office.)

The office dealt with a huge variety of consumer problems, some of which it passed on to the Federal Trade Commission or the Consumer Product Safety Commission. To help consumers and industries settle complaints on a host of products, including furniture, automobiles, and refrigerators, the office established consumer action panels. These also encouraged the industries to police themselves.

One approach to preventing and solving consumer problems was getting information to the public. The office established the Consumer Information Center as a central distribution point for free and low-cost government publications on health, safety, housing, and money management. One of Elizabeth's former Harvard roommates served as consumer education director and directed the creation of a curriculum for elementary through high school.

7

Consuming Interests

One of the functions of the President's Committee on Consumer Interests was to sell its programs to Congress. One day when testifying before the House Appropriations Committee, Virginia Knauer had to leave before completing her statement and taking questions. Elizabeth took her boss's place. The congressman presiding called a recess, but he neglected to turn off the microphone. Those attending heard him say, "Are we going to let this kid take over the hearing?"

Elizabeth was in her thirties, although she looked younger. The congressman's remark may have reflected a common attitude about the role an attractive young woman should play. Like other women, Elizabeth found obstacles to her career—and to simply doing her job—in many places. In one instance, she went to a local men's club for a business meeting with an out-of-town lawyer. What neither knew until a guard refused to let her enter was that the club did not allow women inside its doors. She couldn't go in for the meeting, and the lawyer didn't come out. He waited there for a male staff member to come.

Elizabeth became involved in the women's movement both as

an individual and as a consumer protection advocate. From childhood she had been practicing what came to be called networking, getting to know other people with a common interest, and she made this an important part of her professional life. She sometimes took the lead in organizing women's groups, including Executive Women in Government. Women's special consumer problems were part of Elizabeth's professional concern, and her first speech as part of her job was at a seminar on women and financial credit. At that time women often had difficulty getting loans or credit cards in their own names.

She was to make many more presentations. Mary Hanford says, "When Mrs. Knauer was scheduled for a speech and something came up that was really important, she just handed it to Elizabeth and said, 'Go give this speech.' She would work on it until she got there and give the speech."

Such appearances were to become increasingly frequent and important in her career, and she began to build a reputation as a good speaker. Elizabeth's mother says, "I think speaking is her talent. She enjoys it. It's never something to worry about. She doesn't seem to get nervous, but she does a lot of scribbling and correcting and changing."

Tim Burr, who worked as a management intern for the committee from 1970 to 1972 and later for the Department of Education, says, "She was much less at ease in doing presentations then than she is now. She wasn't a totally comfortable speaker." He wonders if it was partially because "she always wore very heavy glasses."

The office was relatively informal, but, Burr says, "If you wanted to get a decision, you wrote something up and gave it to her. She would check things out before making a decision." In his view, this was partly her legal training and partly her personality. "She spends a lot of time looking at all the points of view on every action before making a decision." He points out that this care prevents mistakes, but, he says, "There were some delays in the whole process as a result."

In later positions she also received criticism for delaying action in order to continue to gather and consider information and opinions. She has attributed this tendency to be exhaustively thorough to her drive for perfection, which, as a cabinet member, she tried to curb.

Such attention to detail takes time. Burr says, "She was always one of the people who were there when you came in the morning and when you left at night."

Her nephew John, who stayed with her the summer of 1974 while working as an intern on Capitol Hill, says, "Her alarm would go off, and fifteen minutes later she would be out of the house." Breakfast at the office was a norm. John notes that as a cabinet secretary with a chauffeur she sometimes used the short ride to work to put on her makeup.

Elizabeth's responsibilities under the Republican administration gained recognition for her. In 1970 she was named Washington's Outstanding Young Woman of the Year. Those same responsibilities made her a target for charges from some consumer activists that she had changed sides by going along with the administration's consumer policies, which emphasized educating consumers and negotiating with companies rather than passing laws to regulate an industry. Other activists continued to consider her a strong consumer advocate who did what she could to sell vital programs to the president and Congress.

Thus began an argument that followed her from those days as a nonpolitical government employee through her political appointments. Critics said she abandoned the ideals of her Great Society beginnings. Supporters answered that she never changed her goals of helping those most in need of help. Still others said she simply acted on the basic Republican philosophy of relying on the private sector and individual effort rather than government intervention to solve problems.

While at the President's Committee on Consumer Interests, she changed her party registration from Democrat to Independent.

In February 1972 the Downtown Washington Jaycees recognized Elizabeth's work by naming her one of two women, the first in twenty-four years, to be honored by the organization's Flemming Awards Commission. Elizabeth said, "Our purpose is to represent the consumer at the highest level of government, being a 'pipeline' from the consumer to the president." She spoke of the importance of educating children and adults to have good shopping habits, saying, "If the young establish these early, they'll follow them all their lives."

That spring she and Virginia Knauer went to see Kansas Senator Robert Dole, chairman of the Republican Party's National Committee, to make a case for a consumer plank in the Republican platform for the upcoming presidential election. When he walked through the door, Elizabeth says, "I just looked up and thought, 'My goodness, he's an attractive man.'" Years later she could remember what she was wearing that day.

Thirteen years older than she and recently divorced, the busy senator wrote her name on a blotter. They met again at the convention and other Washington events, but he did not call her for several months. Later he said he had been concerned about the difference in their ages.

Perhaps he also had heard Elizabeth had been dating a Mississippi congressman. Her long hours did not prevent her from having an active social life. Her family speaks of her bringing home men for them to meet fairly regularly. For more than a decade, hometowners had been asking, "When are you going to get married?" Happy with what she was doing, she refused to be pushed into marriage and advised young women starting their careers to shrug off family and friends' remarks about it being time to walk down the aisle. Publicly and privately she said, "The key to happiness is for a woman to be able to stand on her own two feet and become a person in her own right."

Although her brother John thought she was taking a big risk, she bought her own home, an apartment at the Watergate. A five-minute drive to the White House and ten-minute drive to Capitol Hill, this new building complex became famous as the name for the scandal (the cover-up of an attempted burglary of Democratic campaign offices there in 1972) that forced President Nixon to resign in 1974.

In 1973 the president was to appoint a new commissioner to a seven-year term on the Federal Trade Commission (FTC), the agency responsible for investigating violations of antitrust laws and preventing business from using unfair methods of competition. Virginia Knauer suggested this should be Elizabeth's next step up the career ladder. Their unit, renamed the Office of Consumer Affairs, sent many of the consumer complaints it received on to the FTC for action, so Elizabeth was familiar with many of the issues.

President Nixon recently had appointed another of Knauer's assistants, a Republican, to head the FTC. The law required that the FTC be bipartisan, with no party having more than three of the five commissioners. Elizabeth was a registered Independent, and consumer activists wanted a person with a good record on consumer matters to get the appointment.

Convincing the president to make the appointment turned out to be easier than convincing the Senate to approve it. Elizabeth came under attack from two major forces. Some Democrats feared that appointing an Independent with Republican ties was a trick to allow the president to load the FTC with Republicans. Some consumer groups believed the president's policies favored business and thought Elizabeth would support these at the FTC.

The White House called the staff director of the committee voting on the appointment to ask if Elizabeth Hanford was acceptable. He said no. A little later Elizabeth walked into his office and asked him what she needed to do to gain acceptance. He told her to get consumer activists to endorse her. Knauer urged her to go to the annual convention of the Consumer Federation of America, the nation's largest consumer group, and, in a private meeting, tell influential members the political problems and her view on consumer issues. Elizabeth followed her advice. She also called other leading consumer advocates.

In early August the Consumer Federation opposed her appointment. By mid-August, however, the Senate committee was receiving endorsements from important members of the federation. Both the North Carolina senators, one from each party, also backed Elizabeth. Her chances of being approved rose greatly.

To avoid charges of conflict of interest, of using the position to make money, Elizabeth placed most of her assets, more than $300,000, in a blind trust. That meant she would not control or even know how her money was invested.

Much of the Senate committee's debate on whether to recommend or reject the appointment centered on Elizabeth's role at a White House meeting with five carpet manufacturers during the 1972 presidential campaign. Soon after, three carpet manufacturers contributed $200,000 to the Nixon campaign. Several Nixon aides involved in the campaign had been there. Some wondered if the administration had pressured the carpet industry to contribute to the campaign.

Elizabeth told the committee she went to the meeting because, at the last minute, her boss couldn't. Their office had been urging the carpet manufacturers to set up voluntary standards. She went to hear complaints from and give criticisms to members of the industry, and she had heard no discussion of campaign contributions.

Her testimony on this and other issues impressed the committee. In early October a local newspaper reported that the Senate committee was expected to approve Mary E. Hanford as commissioner. Soon reporters would learn to drop the Mary and call her Elizabeth.

8

The Commissioner Takes a Senator

In her last days at the Office of Consumer Affairs, Elizabeth went to New Jersey to make a speech. When she was almost there, a drunk driver ran into the back of her car. Although shaken, she went on and gave the speech. Two weeks later, suffering from severe back pain, she entered the hospital and spent thirty days in traction. That didn't delay her swearing in, however. Chairman of the FTC Lewis Engman, a former co-worker at the Office of Consumer Affairs, came to the hospital to give her the oath in early December 1973. They celebrated the occasion with a bottle of champagne they had chilled in an ice-filled bedpan.

Elizabeth used the time in bed to bone up on the issues facing the Federal Trade Commission. As a commissioner, she would help enforce such statutes as the Truth in Lending Act and the Fair Credit Reporting Act. Many of the problems the FTC dealt with affected consumers. At that time health care, food, and energy were major areas of concern.

The FTC was an old agency that was undergoing change much

61

as the Office of Consumer Affairs had. One question the FTC addressed regularly was how much the government should regulate business. Engman introduced to the FTC a management system called cost-benefit analysis to help in making decisions. Under this system, the FTC would try to estimate how much it would cost an industry and the economy to make changes and how much its customers and society would benefit from these changes. The FTC compared the estimated costs and benefits.

Elizabeth came to consider cost-benefit analysis an important and desirable tool, but she said that "it must never become a substitute for human judgment or compassion."

She also had been making changes in her private life. A few weeks after the 1972 convention, Senator Bob Dole had called her. She says, "We talked about forty minutes, and it was a *wonderful* conversation. We just seemed to be on the same wavelength, all these mutual interests, lots to talk about." But he didn't ask her out.

Two or three weeks later, he called again. After a long talk, Bob said, "Well, maybe sometime we could have dinner."

"Fine, I'd enjoy that," she replied. But he didn't make a definite date.

On the third call, he asked her to dinner. She says, "He was a little shy. I liked that."

Early in their dating, while he was chairman of the Republican National Committee, she went to meet him to go to dinner. As she waited, she read an article on herself in the evening newspaper that said she was an Independent, a fact she hadn't mentioned to him. She put the paper down when he came in, but he, a news junkie, picked it up.

Elizabeth says, "I remember Bob opening the paper and seeing this article and starting to read it. I said, 'Oh, that's nothing,' because he didn't know I was an Independent. I said, 'Come on, Bob, we're going to be late for dinner. Don't worry about the article.' "

"He said, 'I'm interested. I want to read it.' So he got down to the last, 'Miss Hanford is an Independent.' "

"I can still hear him saying, 'You're a *what?*' "

In 1974, they were seeing each other fairly regularly. *Time* named her one of 200 young leaders of America that year, and he was campaigning for another term in the Senate. Like Elizabeth, he owned a Watergate apartment, but with both working long hours and traveling frequently, neither spent a lot of time at home. The telephone played an important role in the courtship.

Robert Joseph Dole's childhood had been very different from Elizabeth's. Born July 22, 1923, in the little prairie town of Russell, Kansas, he and his brother and two sisters grew up when drought and the Depression combined to make life hard in Kansas. When he was twelve, he began to work as a soda jerk at a drugstore on Main Street. He admired the quick, biting humor of the owners and tried to copy it. As an adult, it would be his trademark. He admired the doctors who came into the drugstore and decided to study medicine.

Active in numerous activities in his small high school, he was also an outstanding student and athlete. When he graduated in 1941, his family was making ends meet by living in the basement of their house and renting the upstairs. A banker lent Bob $300 so he could attend the University of Kansas in Lawrence. There he earned part of his expenses by waiting on tables at his fraternity and, on Saturday mornings, delivering milk in the community.

The United States entered World War II in December 1941. In December 1942 Bob enlisted in the Army's Enlisted Reserve Corps. Two years later the Army sent him to Italy as a second lieutenant. In April 1945, while serving as a platoon leader, he was wounded so severely that, initially, he was paralyzed from the neck down. He gradually regained the use of his legs, but he had several narrow brushes with death and remained hospitalized most of the time for more than two years. He lost one kidney, the use of his right arm and hand, and much of the feeling in his left hand.

While hospitalized in late 1947, he met an occupational therapist named Phyllis Holden. They were married in June 1948. They moved to Arizona because the climate would be good for him, and he attended the University of Arizona. At first Phyllis took notes for him in class and wrote his answers on tests from dictation. Later he got a tape recorder. The next year he transferred to Washburn University in Topeka, Kansas, where he took degrees in history and law. While still a student, he ran as a Republican, the majority party in Russell County, for the Kansas state legislature. He won.

After law school he returned to Russell to practice. In 1960 he ran successfully for the U.S. House of Representatives. Coming from a rural district, he concentrated on agricultural issues.

In 1968, after four terms as a representative, he ran successfully for the Senate. The first letter he wrote as a senator was to his daughter Robin, who had been born in 1954. In 1971 he gained an important post in the Republican Party, chairman of the National Committee. That made him a major influence in the 1972 election campaign, and that is why Elizabeth and her boss had gone to his office to talk to him.

As he and Elizabeth began to grow closer, she took him to Salisbury. Her mother says, "She would bring a boy home, but nothing ever happened—until she brought Bob Dole home." One morning he came into the kitchen with a towel over his damaged right shoulder and said, "Mrs.Hanford, I think you ought to see my problem."

She replied that it wasn't a problem but a badge of honor. Elizabeth has said that the best piece of advice her mother ever gave her was to marry Bob Dole.

Elizabeth continued to date other men after she and Bob began seeing each other. Local newspapers called her one of Washington's most eligible women, and he compared the race for her attention to the Kentucky Derby.

Bob's daughter Robin, then finishing college, remembers that her first inklings of the romance came when her father would get calls after coming home late from the office and announce he was going out to dinner. She wondered why he didn't say with whom or invite her along. When she met Elizabeth, Robin said, "So you're the mystery caller!"

Her father told her of his intention to propose when they were flying back together from Kansas. Robin was amused to see how nervous he was, "to see my father going through what everyone goes through when they fall in love."

By the middle of 1975, the romance was common knowledge. A newspaper gossip columnist known as The Ear wrote that Senator Dole's staff was happy about his "true companionship," for it slowed him down a little. "Never a bad boss, he is apparently less of a taskmaster with a lady on his mind," wrote The Ear.

When the couple announced the engagement in November, many wondered whether Elizabeth would continue to use her maiden name. When one woman asked the couple, the senator answered, "I think we want to have the same name. I don't care if it's Bob Hanford or Elizabeth Dole, we want the same name." Later Elizabeth told a hometown reporter that "there's a lot to be said" for a woman keeping her maiden name in business. For approximately a decade, Elizabeth Hanford Dole was the way her name appeared on most official papers, but by the time she became secretary of labor, Hanford appeared only occasionally.

The alliance of the commissioner, 39, and the senator, 52, on December 6, 1975, was one of the season's most talked about social events. Because both of their fathers were not well, however, the couple decided to have a small wedding ceremony at the Bethlehem Chapel of the Cathedral of St. Peter and St. Paul, commonly known

The bride's parents admire the groom's ring after the wedding ceremony in the Washington Cathedral in 1975.

The bride dances with her brother at the reception.

as the Washington, or National, Cathedral, and a large reception at a downtown club.

One of Elizabeth's childhood friends, Jean Brumley, could not attend, so she called Liddy from Amsterdam to give her good wishes—at six o'clock on her wedding morning.

Elizabeth wore an antique-ivory satin wedding gown with a chapel-length train and a mantilla-style veil of heirloom Belgian lace. Her sister-in-law, Burnell Hanford, was matron of honor, and Robert Ellsworth, assistant defense secretary and a former Kansas congressman, was the best man. The Senate chaplain performed the ceremony. In typical fashion, Elizabeth spent the last few minutes before the ceremony studying the vows. The wedding cake had five tiers and weighed eighty pounds.

During the reception the bridal couple received congratulatory calls from Hubert H. Humphrey, a former Democratic senator and vice-president, and Nelson Rockefeller, former Republican governor of New York whom Gerald Ford had appointed vice-president. Former President Nixon had called to invite them to tea when they were in California.

In a toast Bob Dole said, "The polls close tonight in the closest race I have ever run."

The most light-hearted part of the festivities was a wedding breakfast for seventy people at another club. Each guest received a miniature version of the *Congressional Digest*. It included the guest list and this imitation of an official statement: "I move to amend the Robinson-Patman Act to render the Dole-Hanford merger a combination in the public interest, and not in undue restraint of trade."

Many joked about the joining of the executive and legislative branches of government and the possible conflicts of interests.

The couple left for their honeymoon, but the death of Bob's father brought them back early. Elizabeth met much of her husband's large family at the funeral.

Elizabeth moved into Bob's two-bedroom apartment, and the two went back to work.

Robin Dole says that she gained a friend when her father remarried. "One of the things that I find very important and very special is that she never made any attempt to be my mother. I had a mother. Her effort was to be my friend."

On the first Mother's Day after the wedding, Robin took Elizabeth a card and some flowers. Robin remembers tears coming to Elizabeth's eyes. "She was almost shocked. I am sure she hadn't even thought of herself in this role." Before long, they would have another relationship, players on Bob Dole's political team.

9

A Campaign, Two Careers, Some Conflicts

Shortly after Elizabeth and Bob were married, the 1976 presidential race began. For months President Gerald R. Ford and former California governor Ronald Reagan competed in the primaries for the Republican nomination. When the convention started in August, President Ford's nomination was a virtual certainty, but he had not selected a running mate.

Two weeks before the convention, the White House asked Bob Dole and a number of others to submit their financial and medical records.

July was a hectic time at the FTC, and Elizabeth looked forward to going on vacation after the convention in Kansas City, Missouri, for the Doles did not consider his nomination likely. An old friend remembers Elizabeth pointing out to a television interviewer at the convention that she was a registered Independent, not a Republican.

Elizabeth says she doesn't remember when she officially became a Republican and adds, "Being a Southern Democrat was the same as being a Republican. It was sort of the same philosophy. It just took me a little while to get there."

After President Ford received the party nomination, he held late-night discussions on possible vice-presidential candidates with Governor Reagan, for his backers could provide considerable help during the campaign. The defeated candidate didn't want to run for vice-president, but he wanted a candidate acceptable to him and his followers on the party's right.

Early the next morning the Doles heard voices outside their hotel room. The press had come to check on strong rumors that Bob Dole was to be Ford's running mate. When the president called to ask Bob to run with him, it took the senator only a moment to answer yes. The Secret Service soon arrived to protect the candidate and his wife, who received the code names Ramrod and Rainbow.

When the campaign began, the Democratic candidates, Jimmy Carter and Walter Mondale, were far ahead in the polls. The Republican team began trying to catch up immediately. They went from the convention to a rally in Bob's nearby hometown. Elizabeth suddenly found herself in the role of candidate's wife. That usually meant being seen and not heard or at least not heard voicing any political opinions.

Bob's candidacy affected Elizabeth's status at the FTC. Commissioners were not supposed to play an active public role in presidential campaigns. No other commissioner had been married to a national candidate, so no one had faced the situation before. Some said she should resign. Some said a wife should not have to leave her position because of that of her husband.

Shortly before announcing her decision, Elizabeth pointed out the law did not require her to resign, but added, "The question is, is it right or proper to keep on? There's no precedent for this decision, so it's going to be a law-making one."

Elizabeth found a path between the extremes. She took a leave of absence.

The couple and numerous official and unofficial advisers tried to decide what her duties in the campaign would be. Her husband wanted her to campaign with him as he traveled around the country. Many women urged her to use her considerable knowledge of issues and experience as a speaker to campaign for the ticket on her own. They compromised. Ramrod and Rainbow traveled together as much as possible, but they spoke to or met with different groups in each city.

Many of Elizabeth's events were the ceremonial ones that candidates' wives traditionally had taken care of, but she studied her husband's positions so she could speak for him on the issues whenever she had an opportunity. Elizabeth also expressed her own views, particularly on the importance of women being able to stand

Best friends chat in the Hanfords' den during the 1976 presidential campaign.

on their own feet. Robin, just out of college, handled events where she would not have to discuss issues.

Although she had always liked to be well-prepared, Elizabeth found she had to adapt to constant surprises. Schedules and events often changed at the last minute. She also found that she liked campaigning, that she drew energy and satisfaction from the crowds and the individuals she met. Her husband called her his "Southern strategy," a joking comparison to President Nixon's plan for winning the South in 1972.

In 1960 the televised debate between presidential candidates John F. Kennedy and Richard M. Nixon had proved key to the election. In 1976, the candidates for the vice-presidency debated on television for the first time. Elizabeth worried that the other elements of the campaign left Bob too little time to prepare properly. Known for his quick, stinging wit, he went on determined to make a few strong points, and he used strong words to do it. Mondale, and many others, called him the Republican ticket's hatchet man.

Later, one of the senator's aides, Bill Wohlford, indicated to *Newsweek* that Elizabeth told Bob his humor was so biting it was harming him as well as his targets. Wohlford said, "Since Elizabeth, the thrust of his stories tends to be turned back on himself. He's more gracious, less tart."

The Doles joined the Fords at the White House to watch the returns coming in. When they saw that Carter, a Georgian, had taken the South, they went home.

Elizabeth was amazed at how unemotional her husband of less than a year seemed about the defeat. She later told a *Newsweek* reporter, "The next day he just said, 'OK, we didn't make it,' and that was that." He did suggest asking for a recount in some states where the votes were very close, but President Ford dismissed the idea.

Bob went back to the Senate and Elizabeth went back to the Federal Trade Commission. Whenever she could, she attended the

Senate Wives Red Cross meetings. Each Tuesday they knitted items for hospitalized veterans or made such things as puppets for sick children.

Sometimes the commissioner, serving in the executive branch, and the senator, serving in the legislative branch, found themselves opposing one another. In a case concerning the distribution rights of independent bottlers, Elizabeth wrote the opinion for the FTC, and Bob was one of the senators who voted to overturn it.

One of their most public disagreements was over the establishment of a consumer protection agency. She argued that it would bring together more than two dozen separate and sometimes overlapping consumer offices. He said it would be expensive and likely to regulate business needlessly. They gave their opinions before business groups and debated their points on a morning television news program. The public rarely had seen a political husband and wife disagree on policy. Their differences attracted much attention to them and the issue.

Often using humor to soften the disagreement, Bob said after one debate, "I'll be in so much hot water tonight they'll be able to name a tea bag after me."

One of the issues at the FTC in which Elizabeth took special interest was health care for the elderly, particularly those with little money. She attempted to get the commission to start an investigation of nursing homes, and she called for a study of the state laws on insurance for those who wished to supplement Medicare. She had some personal insight into the problems of the elderly, for her beloved grandmother had entered a nursing home. Also, on Sundays Elizabeth visited elderly people who could not leave their homes or who lived in nursing homes.

She viewed government regulation and support as only part of the solution to older citizens' health-care problems. Speaking to the Indiana Governor's Conference on Aging in 1978 she said, "Government cannot and should not do it all; private funds and volunteers are needed to provide these services—and that means a responsibility for each of us in our own communities."

In some speeches she stressed her concern for "protecting special groups of consumers who need—as well as deserve—a stronger helping hand from the government. I am, of course, speaking of such groups as children, the elderly, the poor, and the disadvantaged. Many of these consumers lack buying sophistication, or their access to the marketplace may be restricted, or their ability to comparison shop is limited. Frequently, they find it hard to make informed choices in a free market. In short, they suffer more harshly than anyone else from deceptive advertising and marketing techniques, shoddy goods, or discriminatory credit practices." She had made similar statements while working with the Office of Consumer Affairs, and she was to express concern for these groups as a cabinet officer.

For years she had been a backer of the Equal Rights Amendment and other measures to obtain equality for women. At the FTC she maintained her special interest in women's issues, such as receiving fair consideration for credit cards and loans.

During a 1977 FTC workshop for women in business, she said, "There was a time when it was said in Washington—as in many other parts of the country—that a woman had to work twice as hard as a man in order to get half as far. Unfortunately, that's sometimes still the case. But those days are changing."

She pointed out, "Women, I understand, make up 39 percent of the total work force but only 5 percent of the managers, proprietors, and officials earning more than $10,000 a year. At higher salary levels—$25,000 a year or more—women only account for 2.3 percent of such earners."

The law could not solve all of the problems, she said. "Attitudes are still very much a part of the continuing barriers to full equality of opportunity.

"Part of the change—perhaps the largest part—must still come on the other side, among those—both men and women—who cling to notions that men should dominate the society. That is an effort that requires the continuing devotion of us all, and let us recognize that many of our strongest allies in this effort are often our male counterparts."

In October 1978, North Carolina newspapers reported Elizabeth was considering running for the eighth district congressional seat. One wrote that she was registered as an Independent in Salisbury but that if she decided to run, it would be as a Republican. She did not run.

In late 1978 her father died at age eighty-five. She says, "He was a wonderfully loving father [and] the grief was just incredible." In going over his affairs, she discovered that he had not raised the rent for elderly tenants living in apartments he owned for many years.

As the 1980 presidential campaign and Bob's bid for the Republican nomination approached, Elizabeth again faced the question of how her husband's career would affect hers. This time Elizabeth resigned to devote all her efforts to the campaign. They both traveled a lot, and when they were at home, they spent their evenings at political events—often two or three a night. Sometimes the only time they saw each other for two or three days would be at those events. Washington called them the "power couple."

Elizabeth dislikes the phrase, which has continued to follow them over the years. She says, "I cringe at that because—there can be more than one meaning—it's as though you are grasping for power. I don't look at life that way."

Bob's try for the Republican nomination ended the next spring as Ronald Reagan beat out other contenders in the primaries. Bob joked that he withdrew from the race when Elizabeth passed him the polls.

He decided to run for re-election to the Senate. Elizabeth's choice was less obvious. She had said for years that she had no career blueprint. During the 1976 campaign she said, "I just took the best opportunity I saw when I turned a corner. That's why I think it's important for a woman to get a good education. When the options turn up, she's prepared to choose one she wants."

At this corner, Elizabeth chose to work with Ronald Reagan's presidential campaign. Looking back she says, "It all just sort of flowed. There was no time to stop and think, 'All right, I'm at a crossroads.' "

Still, she acknowledges that her days of coming up through the ranks as a civil servant were over. She says, "As I became more involved in the political world with Bob, I was at a point where you were going to serve at the pleasure of the president or you weren't going to serve."

10

Serving the President

In 1980 Ronald Reagan and his vice-presidential candidate, George Bush, campaigned against President Jimmy Carter and Vice-President Walter Mondale. Elizabeth set up such voter groups as Blacks for Reagan-Bush and Women for Reagan-Bush and then became part of a so-called truth squad. Squad members' role, she said, was "going in before Carter to suggest questions for the press, going in after he left to set the record straight."

After the election, President-elect Reagan appointed Elizabeth director of the human services group, one of the planning groups helping him prepare to take office. Rumors circulated that he might appoint Elizabeth to a cabinet office.

She *was* the first woman he appointed, but the position was head of the White House Office of Public Liaison. Some said she got the position because the administration wanted to assure her husband's support in the Senate. Some said she got it in spite of him, for he did not always agree with Ronald Reagan and George Bush. Others noted she had earned it with her work during the campaign and the transition.

The job began with a deluge of work. Shortly, after she took the position Bob became ill in the night. She says, "I was the one who took him to the hospital. He never complains about anything. When he woke up and said, 'Something is wrong,' I knew something terrible was wrong." During a seven-hour surgery, doctors removed a stone from his remaining kidney. He recovered well.

Despite the twin pressures of her husband's illness and a new job, she doesn't remember that as a difficult time. Elizabeth says, "My faith means a lot to me. I don't feel that I have to do it all on my own. I think I can face challenging situations and feel there's a source of strength beyond myself, that it's not all just on my shoulders."

She adds, "I'm a pretty optimistic person. I don't let things get me down for too long." Friends and reporters long have commented on her persistent cheerfulness and optimism, the former considering these a vital part of her personality and the latter wondering if they are genuine.

Over the years Elizabeth and Bob had learned to cope with the pressures of their respective jobs by limiting conversation about their work at home. They had little time away from their offices, and they needed that time to relax. They tried to make their home an oasis from the turmoil at work. Elizabeth often spoke of "compartmentalizing" their professional and private lives. This became even more important as Elizabeth moved up in the executive and Bob in the legislative branch. Some matters they simply didn't discuss, particularly when policies or legislation were still being formed in their respective government branches. In some instances, of course, they could not resist holding small private debates in which they tried to change each other's opinions.

They had been aware that their careers might cause conflicts when they married, so they had made an effort to overcome them. Each understood the importance and demands of the other's work, and each supported the other. Bob occasionally helped at home by doing such things as cooking dinner—if it could be a one-ingredient meal, such as hot dogs. They tested various frozen dinners as these came on the market.

Shortly after Elizabeth accepted the appointment, and at other times, interviewers asked her whether she planned to have children. A typical answer was, "If it happens we'd be delighted. It would be great." She points out how close she has been to her two nephews, John and Jody, and how well she gets along with her stepdaughter, Robin.

She preferred to talk to reporters about her work rather than her private life. She described Public Liaison's function as "providing the opportunity for different groups in our society to have input and make their concerns known at the highest levels of government." Heading a staff of thirty-two, she reported to chief-of-staff James Baker but had access to President Reagan, too.

To a great extent, her job involved trying to sell the president's policies to special-interest groups, mostly national organizations with deep concerns about one or two issues and general concerns about others. Many of the groups supported the president's policies. Many times, however, Elizabeth had to try to build bridges to groups charging that the administration was neglecting social needs in favor of defense and business interests. If she couldn't gain support for a measure, she tried to control the damage.

Some of Elizabeth's old friends and allies were angry because the president opposed the Equal Rights Amendment (ERA). They considered the administration's other steps to promote equal rights inadequate—or worse. Elizabeth had voiced support for the amendment in the past. Now some ERA backers criticized her for not taking a public stand for ERA. She looked for compromises. She spearheaded new administration efforts through the White House Coordinating Council on Women, but, for the most part, the women's movement continued to condemn the administration's efforts.

Pat Reuss, legislative director of the Women's Equity Action

League, defended Elizabeth. Reuss said that women's groups expected Elizabeth to accomplish more for women's rights than any woman on that White House staff could.

Another question frequently raised was how much power the lone woman on the senior White House staff had. In May 1982, for example, *Newsweek* carried an article under the headline: "Elizabeth Dole: White House Shutout." Elizabeth answered claims that she had little influence by saying that she had as much access and input to the president and his key staff as other assistants did. Otherwise she would not have found the job satisfying.

Much of her input was based on gathering opinions about current issues from nongovernmental organizations. She was, in effect, testing the political winds. When the administration made policies, she then talked to representatives of the appropriate organizations about these to gain their support or lessen their opposition. She also helped the administration plan campaigns, including telephone calls and letters to key persons, for bills the administration wanted Congress to pass.

Sometimes the head of Public Liaison directed her own campaigns for bills at the new chairman of the important Senate Finance Committee, Senator Bob Dole. Elizabeth didn't always win, and she didn't always try very hard. Speaking of differences in the White House and his positions, Bob said, "She might raise it with me to indicate that people she works with have a different position, but she has to do her thing and I have to do my thing."

Although her husband supported most administration measures, he considered Kansas voters, not the president, his boss. When the administration wanted to cut the food stamp program by $2.3 billion, for example, Bob proposed a much smaller cut of $700 million.

As usual, both the Doles were working very hard. They continued to postpone buying a house, although they had joined with other family members to buy a condo in Bal Harbour, Florida, as a place to relax for a few days on winter breaks.

On a typical day, Elizabeth got up at 6:00 A.M. and left their Watergate apartment before 7:00 A.M., Bob's rising time, to drive to the White House. There she had breakfast and read newspapers before going to an 8:00 A.M. meeting with other senior presidential staff members. At 9:00 A.M. she would meet with her own staff. Much of the rest of her day would be filled with meetings with organizations' representatives (including going with them to meet briefly with the president), meetings with various individuals or on current problems, and studying papers to prepare for other meetings. In her two years in this job she met with some 2,000 groups and gave some 200 speeches.

Later, as secretary of labor, she would say, "Meetings can chew up a lot of time."

She would leave her office in the West Wing of the White House about twelve hours after she arrived. If she got home in time, she would watch the evening news while riding an exercise bicycle. Many evenings she and Bob both had work-related dinners or parties to attend. Much of the time they had a person come in several half days a week to clean the apartment and do some cooking. Elizabeth studied books on time management, a favorite one being Alex Mackenzie's *The Time Trap*. She made daily to-do lists.

In spite of the hectic schedule, Elizabeth found time to take care of personal matters, including renewing a childhood friendship. It started when Elizabeth's uncle, Joe Cathey, drove into a gas station in a town near Salisbury. A woman working there realized he was Elizabeth's uncle and said, "I was in school with her, and I'd love to write her, but she wouldn't have time to read a letter from me."

He replied, "You write her, and I know you'll hear from her."

The woman sent Elizabeth an afghan she had crocheted and wrote, in part, "I never could understand why you traded your sandwiches for my peanut butter sandwiches at school." She could hardly believe it when one day her boss called her to come to the phone to take a call from the White House.

Elizabeth and the old friend corresponded, and the woman mentioned that she had always wanted to come to Washington but didn't have the money. Then Elizabeth learned the woman had cancer.

Elizabeth invited the woman and her family to come to Washington for a weekend and flew them in. Bob took them to a French restaurant, where he amazed the guests by eating ten courses. On Sunday, Elizabeth planned to take her visitors to church, but Bob said, "You go to church all the time, don't you?" When they said yes, he said, "Is there anything up here you'd like to see you haven't seen?"Again they said yes. The group decided to go sightseeing instead of to church that Sunday.

Not long after that, the woman told Elizabeth she was stopping cancer therapy because the family couldn't afford it. Elizabeth said, "Don't you dare cut those. You send the bills to me, and I am going to pay for them." She did, but the treatments did not save the woman's life.

Elizabeth had grown up in a family attaching great importance to religion. In her childhood, Sunday was God's day. Her grandmother, who practiced her faith with word and deed, was Elizabeth's role model. When Cora Cathey's son died following a car accident caused by a drunken driver, she donated his insurance money to establish a mission in Pakistan.

After leaving Salisbury, Elizabeth gradually put less emphasis on religion, and Sunday often became a work day. As she told a women's group at Salisbury's First United Methodist Church in 1984, her life seemed "threatened with spiritual starvation." She felt consumed by her career and her desire for perfection.

"A perfectionist may take it to extremes, making it tough on your family, friends, fellow workers and self," she said. She began to go to Monday night spiritual growth meetings sponsored by the

Church of the Saviour, known for its dedication to improving the lives of the poor, after her day at the White House. One member of the group, Jennifer (Jenna) Dorn, has served as a member of Elizabeth's staff at Transportation, Labor, and the American Red Cross.

When President Reagan offered her the job of secretary of transportation, she discussed it with the Monday night group as well as her family before accepting the offer.

Nephew John, who had studied economics before becoming a Methodist minister, realized the difficulty of mastering the complex and controversial questions with which the Department of Transportation (DOT) was dealing. He believes that few people, even those with experience in the special field, are ready to take over a cabinet department. He said to her, "Do you really think this is the best thing?"

She did, and he says, "She certainly proved any doubts I had to be misplaced. She stepped in with her administrative abilities and her communications skills, her ability to work so well with people and to pull together a team."

Elizabeth admits she found the idea of being secretary of transportation, a position no woman had held, interesting partly because of the difficulties. She says, "There's something challenging and appealing about going into a situation that's not the easiest and making it work."

11

Closing the Gender Gap

In announcing Elizabeth's appointment to the cabinet during a press conference on January 6, 1983, President Reagan said she "has been performing magnificently as my assistant for public liaison at the White House."

Bob issued a two-word press release. It said, "Excellent choice." For her to become Madam Secretary, however, other senators would have to agree—or at least to confirm her appointment.

After the press conference, Elizabeth returned to her office and spent two hours calling those she had worked with in the past and those she would be working with in her new position.

The next morning an editorial in the *Washington Post* pointed out how demanding and complex the position had become and what some of the critical issues were, including improving highways, training air traffic controllers, and making cars safer. The editorial called Elizabeth "accomplished and skilled" and said "her legal, managerial, political and government experience should stand her in good stead as head of one of the largest and most diverse of the federal agencies."

Some reporters wrote that the appointment helped the White House avoid an awkward situation. An article in *The New York Times* said, "She has found herself defending the Administration's economic policies when her husband, Senator Bob Dole, was on the other end of Pennsylvania Avenue publicly criticizing the same policies and offering alternatives." This conflict was important because Bob seemed ready to run for the presidency in 1984 if President Reagan didn't.

Bob made a joke of the differences between the views of the Dole at the White House and the Dole on Capitol Hill. When he and Elizabeth spoke to the same group, he sometimes began by saying, "Now that Elizabeth has given you the administration line, let me tell you what is really happening."

Appointing Elizabeth helped the president with another special problem, the political gender gap. Polls showed that more men than women favored the Republican Party and supported President Reagan.

Most women's organizations applauded Elizabeth's appointment. Kathy Wilson, president of the National Women's Political Caucus, said, "We're high on her. She's our ally at the White House."

With confirmation of the appointment virtually certain and Elizabeth preparing to leave the White House, *Washington Post* reporter Elisabeth Bumiller wrote an article about Elizabeth's status there. Many people had considered the Public Liaison position a difficult one, and Bumiller wrote, "Dole listened to complaints— and there were a lot—of women, blacks, veterans, the handicapped, Indians, business leaders, farmers and so on. She took a lot of abuse, but found few inside people willing to listen to her."

Some White House staff members told the reporter Elizabeth had a hard time setting priorities and that she spent too much time on research. Chief-of-staff James Baker, however, called her "an extraordinarily competent person."

Elizabeth studied for the new position with her usual thoroughness—reading widely with much underlining, taking notes, questioning staff members, and consulting with former Transportation secretaries and experts.

When she went before the Senate Commerce Committee to gain approval of the appointment, her husband introduced her. During the hearing, he rephrased Nathan Hale's famous final words, saying, "I regret that I have but one wife to give to my country's infrastructure."

One senator raised the question of conflict of interest between Senator Dole and Secretary Dole. Elizabeth replied, "It's a matter of professional integrity. My husband and I have talked this over. We see no problem. We have no hesitation about compartmentalizing."

The Senate approved the appointment by a vote of ninety-seven to nothing, and on February 7, 1983, Supreme Court Associate Justice Sandra Day O'Connor, the first woman to sit on the Supreme Court, gave Elizabeth the oath of office at the White House. Mary Hanford, whom Elizabeth calls "my Cabinet, my confidante, and my sounding board," held Cora Cathey's bible as Elizabeth took the oath.

She became the seventh woman to serve in the cabinet and the first to head a branch of the armed services, for the Coast Guard falls under the DOT. Her department's budget was $27 billion.

The new cabinet officer made safety a dominant theme and studied possible ways of saving lives in various forms of transportation. She was impressed with research indicating that placing brake lights in the rear windows of cars would reduce rear-end crashes. She reversed the decision made by the previous secretary and required that rear-window brake lights become standard equipment for 1986 vehicles.

Shortly thereafter, she came out in favor of air bags even though the previous secretary had gone to the Supreme Court to resist requiring automakers to put these and other passive restraints, automatic safety belts, in new cars.

Many observers saw this safety issue as a test of her willingness to stand up for her beliefs in consumers' rights as she had at the Office of Consumer Affairs and at the Federal Trade Commission. Consumer advocate Ralph Nader said her decision "will either confirm the impression that Elizabeth Dole is not willing to stand up for victims against power or it will make Elizabeth Dole the most courageous Cabinet secretary in the Reagan administration."

The Supreme Court ruled against the previous secretary and ordered more study on the need for passive restraints. Elizabeth sought a solution that would gain the president's approval and would meet both immediate and long-term needs. She says, "It was

Vice-President George Bush, Secretary Dole, and President Ronald Reagan share the platform as she announces a new policy.

probably the toughest public policy issue I've ever dealt with. We put together a very intricate rule that was designed to save as many lives as possible as quickly as possible."

Under the DOT plan, all 1990 automobile models would have to have some type of approved automatic passenger restraints, unless two-thirds of the nation's people lived in states with stiff safety-belt laws. The plan encouraged people to use the safety belts already available in cars and crucial in rear-end and rollover crashes. It also encouraged manufacturers to produce air bags for protection in front and side crashes. The DOT designed Rule 208 to produce competition between those favoring safety-belt laws and those favoring air bags and automatic belts.

As Elizabeth saw it, the public couldn't lose. States would be passing laws requiring seat belts immediately, and laws requiring passive restraints would go into effect later when the automakers had improved technology. To encourage automakers to offer air bags as an option, she had bags put into 5,000 government-owned cars, including her own official car, a Lincoln.

As in most compromises, Rule 208 displeased and pleased some people on both sides. For example, the executive director of the Center for Auto Safety accused her of caving in to the auto companies. On the other hand, a Republican senator, a strong safety advocate, said, "I was amazed she could sell that to the administration."

In 1984, only fourteen out of one hundred people wore safety belts, and not one state had a law requiring it. In 1990, almost half did. Elizabeth was able to say of the plan she devised, "It's worked the way we intended it to. Thirty-six states have safety belt laws covering eighty-eight percent of the American population."

In early 1991 Elizabeth called her action on auto safety "the matter that I'm prouder of than anything else in my twenty-five years of government." Over the years she received many awards, but the one she valued most highly was the 1989 National Safety Council's Distinguished Service to Safety Award.

Elizabeth moved ahead with other measures, including getting drunk drivers off the road and improving air safety.

Almost as soon as she took office, she asked about the status of women at DOT, traditionally male territory. Only nineteen percent of the employees were women. Elizabeth remembered her early years of job hunting when the first question most bosses asked women was, "Can you type?" She had campaigned for better jobs for women throughout her career, and now she had more control than ever before. She launched a program to help women advance. By 1986, twenty-three percent of DOT's personnel were women, and the number in managerial positions had doubled. Elizabeth also

Secretary Dole speaks during a rally on the Capitol steps to promote auto safety by raising the drinking age to twenty-one.

saw to it that DOT opened a women's exercise room and a child day-care center.

Partially because she was one of the few women in a high administration job, the new secretary of transportation attracted more and more national attention. Often the press devoted almost as many words to her personal qualities as her professional capabilities. In July 1983 *Life* carried a profile that called her "as sweet as shoofly pie" and said that "she has made astonishingly few enemies."

The writer asked Elizabeth about her reputation for attention to detail. She said, "I am a meticulous person, and I like to understand the details. Maybe it's the lawyer in me." She reflected on her drive for perfection, which her new position had forced her to curb, and said, "There's just not enough time in my life anymore. I think there is a point where you have to be willing to accept less than perfect, whether it's in yourself or in others."

Bob put it this way, "Her total desire to do everything right is almost a negative. She will find out that by the time you get rid of one hot potato, there are three more waiting in the outer office."

Once again the twelve-hour day was the norm. Elizabeth would get to the office about 8:15 A.M. and preside over a staff meeting at 8:30. There staff members would look at any overnight events and go over the day's agenda. Once or twice a week Elizabeth would have cabinet meetings. Much of her day would be spent in meetings with staff members, special task forces on the various forms of transportation with which DOT dealt, and advisory committees.

Elizabeth had not abandoned her long-time habit of asking advice from many sources. She said, "What you always do before you make a decision is consult. The best public policy is made when you are listening to people who are going to be impacted. Then, once a policy is determined, you call on them to help you sell it."

Secretary Dole became an administration spokeswoman. People began to mention her as a running mate with President

Reagan in 1984, but she told a reporter flatly, "That's not in the realm of possibility."

That didn't stop the rumors, and the Doles often joked about whether one or both would run for President in 1984 if President Reagan did not. Bob was famous for his quick wit, particularly one-liners, but Elizabeth liked to plan her jokes. More and more they formed a comedy team, usually poking fun at each other and themselves.

At an annual press dinner where the speakers' goal was to prompt laughter, Bob announced, "Dole will not be a candidate for president in 1984."

Elizabeth jumped up and shouted, "Speak for yourself, sweetheart."

A few weeks later, Bob told those attending a dinner honoring his wife that he was willing to be "the first man."

The Doles also used humor when they found themselves on different sides of issues. In early 1984 Elizabeth testified before Bob's Senate Finance Committee on taxes on trucks. As the hearing began, she joked that she "hoped we can come to a quick agreement on this matter before all three houses."

When she agreed with a senator who disapproved of exempting gasohol from federal gasoline and diesel taxes, Bob said, "She agrees with you, and you're both wrong."

The pair often said that he was in charge of loopholes and she was in charge of potholes.

"Power couple" had become a standard label for them, and Elizabeth played an increasingly important role in selling the Reagan administration's policies. She had many personal opportunities to study the problems of the airlines, which the public was criticizing for flight delays, as she flew around the country making speeches. She chose to fly on commercial airlines rather than use the costlier but more convenient government aircraft.

The senator said of the administration, "If they're smart, they'll just buy her a road map and an airplane and say, 'See you after the election.' "

When the Democrats nominated the first female vice-presidential candidate, Geraldine Ferraro, in 1984, the Republicans came under additional pressure to close the gender gap. President Reagan chose George Bush as his running mate again, but the president asked Elizabeth to speak to the Republican convention during prime television time. One of her themes was the administration's attempts to give women new opportunities.

Elizabeth had laryngitis the day before her speech, and Bob stood in for her at a reception for cabinet women. He said, "I was one of the honored ladies. No one seemed to know the difference."

The senator and the secretary attracted a great deal of attention at the convention considering neither was a candidate. Many attendees wore buttons bearing the slogan "Dole-Dole '88," and everyone knew their hotel room number—1988.

12

A Dole for President?

Elizabeth became a top Republican fundraiser as the Reagan-Bush ticket battled the Mondale-Ferraro ticket in 1984. She campaigned for Republicans in House and Senate races as well as for the national ticket. Sometimes she attended campaign events in four or five towns in a state on one day and then did the same in a neighboring state the next day. She spoke at lunches and dinners, rallies, and press conferences. In some cases she made formal speeches from a prepared text, but often she spoke from notes she put on five-by-seven-inch cards or simply made remarks that fit the occasion.

Known for being a perfectionist about her appearance as well as her work, Elizabeth surprised some by traveling with only one hanging bag that she could carry on. Explaining how she managed, she said, "I coordinate, so you can crisscross blouses and skirts, wear it in the day, and it's also dressy enough, if you change the accessories, to wear at night—sort of a survival approach. Otherwise you'd never make it." She carried a shoulder purse. She had stopped carrying clutch purses after finding holding one extremely inconvenient while going up and down ladders on a Coast Guard cutter.

As in 1980, the Republicans won both the presidency and a majority of seats in the Senate. On November 29, Republican senators elected Bob Dole majority leader.

To mark the occasion, Elizabeth gave him a black and gray miniature schnauzer she named Leader. He had been living on borrowed time at a Humane Society kennel. She had planned the dog as a Christmas gift, but instead she presented it at the press conference following Bob's election as majority leader.

"This is an indication of where my leadership is going," Bob joked. He said the dog was housebroken but not Senate-broken.

Elizabeth had wanted to get a pet for some time, but the amount of traveling she and Bob did made it difficult to care for one. She decided to find someone to share ownership, and did. Nevertheless, Leader spent a good deal of time in Bob's Senate offices and in Elizabeth's offices at the Department of Transportation.

Bob and Elizabeth sometimes made wagers to determine who would walk the dog. When Duke and Kansas played each other, Leader's followers each bet on their home teams. Elizabeth said, "Whoever loses has to take the last shift in walking Leader . . . for the month of April—and that's tough duty."

She faced "tough duty" at the Department of Transportation, too. Elizabeth had made safety a major concern. One of her biggest struggles was over giving unexpected drug tests to those responsible for operating transportation equipment. She says, "Hardly anyone supported me on going forward on random drug testing. I felt very strongly that if an air traffic controller or a person inspecting the railroad is on drugs, then that is absolutely intolerable."

At the time she thought, "No matter how many people oppose me on this, when people are directing traffic in the air and literally hundreds of people could be killed if their judgment is off, no one can tell me it isn't right to test."

She adds, "The random drug testing for safety and security

purposes is now pretty well accepted. It wasn't then. We were the first department outside of the military to do it.

"It's such a wonderful feeling when I'm on the side of the angels," she says. "Let 'er roll, no matter what the barriers. It can't always be that way. You can't always have that assurance, no doubt in your mind, that this is right. But when you have that feeling, it's a wonderful inspiration to drive forward."

Nevertheless, some said she was not matching actions with words in all forms of transportation. In August 1985 *Washington Post* reporter Douglas Feaver interviewed Elizabeth and several of her critics about her work at the department.

Consumer and safety advocate Ralph Nader, who had hoped for an immediate move to air bags, said, "I would call her a weak,

Senator Dole and Secretary Dole make an unusual joint appearance on Capitol Hill after a hearing in early 1984.

Leader gets a prominent place in a portrait of the Doles.

ineffectual secretary of transportation with good, basic instincts that would require a progressive president to nurture," and he added, "She does not like conflict or confrontations." Nader indicated that he thought she would have to meet ideologues in the administration head-on.

Her response was that "the goal is to reach the goal, and there are times when you're going to have to reflect other persons' views and thoughts and try to reach a compromise."

Reporter Feaver wrote that critics within DOT and those with whom it worked complained that regulations, reports, and even press releases stalled in the secretary's office, a charge she denied. The reporter indicated that many of the complaints about slow action at DOT dated back to before Elizabeth was in the job and that the complexity of the issues and the determination of special-interest groups made movement extremely difficult.

He also wrote, "When Dole applies her personal charm to a problem—always after extensive preparation to guard against surprises—she is formidable." He told how she had won over a Democratic congressman who had criticized DOT's handling of the sale of Conrail, one of the biggest and longest lasting problems DOT faced in the 1980s.

Put together from several failed companies in the 1970s, federally chartered Conrail had been costing the government millions of dollars. Before Elizabeth became secretary of transportation, Congress had ordered DOT to sell it. In February 1985, Elizabeth accepted the best offer, but she couldn't get the bill approving the sale to the Senate floor for a vote. She accused Bob, the person who could get it there, of trying so hard to be fair he was being unfair to her department. When the bill finally received Senate approval in December, it met opposition in the House. The company withdrew its offer.

In September 1986, the key congressional committee agreed

that DOT could sell the railroad through selling shares to whoever would buy. That began in early 1987.

Deregulation (doing away with laws governing business operations) and privatization (selling government-owned operations to industry) were two themes of the Reagan administration that Elizabeth emphasized. One case involved encouraging the development of an industry to launch commercial satellites. The National Aeronautics and Space Administration (NASA) was launching both the government's and industry's satellites. Elizabeth argued that companies with commercial satellites were receiving "discount fares" from the government, thereby preventing private companies from trying to compete with NASA.

When the space shuttle Challenger exploded and fell into the sea in January 1986, NASA postponed launching commercial satellites. Those who wanted satellites launched on schedule had to take their business outside the United States. Elizabeth's position gained support. In mid-1987 she gave preliminary government approval for the nation's first launch by a private company.

Occasionally the Doles traveled together on government business. In 1985, for example, they went to Japan and China together but with separate agendas. He headed a group of senators concerned with trade issues, and she headed a DOT group. She says, "It was very challenging having these two going at once. It was a very hectic trip." In China she had no counterpart. She had to negotiate technical assistance agreements with five departments, each dealing with different areas of transportation.

With both Doles having overflowing work schedules, they tried to reserve Sundays as a time to be together and with their family and friends, often going to brunch after church. They also made time for church work, particularly helping the elderly.

Describing their Sunday afternoons, Bob said, "Around two o'clock we generally go home and read the papers and watch the Sunday news shows. I like to get out in the sun on the patio;

Elizabeth will read or make phone calls. She can't sit still. I can go outside and do nothing, but when she's outside she has a pile of papers or books."

Reading the Bible or other religious materials is a regular part of Elizabeth's day. Her nephew John, a minister working in a senator's office, remembers that during a family tour of England, she sometimes would not talk to them in the van in the morning until she completed her daily reading. At other times, however, the secretary of transportation did her share of the driving.

John tells how reading the Scriptures changed the way she celebrates her birthday. He says, "She read the part where Jesus said when you are having a party, don't go out and invite the rich and famous, the people who can return the favor to you. Rather go out and invite the poor and the lame and others who cannot."

During a trip to China in 1985, Secretary Dole made a new friend at the Great Wall.

Every year her staff threw her a birthday party, but she decided to find people in need and give them a party. Bob, whose birthday comes a week before hers, joined in. A friend who worked with the Church of the Saviour helped her find a group of older people and get an idea of a gift each would enjoy. Elizabeth went out, John says, and carefully picked out gifts.

The party was such a success, they gave another the next year. John attended that one. He says, "It was wonderful to see the rapport. Liddy would go from table to table with that warmth of hers and cheer up people and get them all excited."

In 1987, Elizabeth planned to celebrate her fifty-first birthday in Salisbury by giving a party for children from the Nazareth Children's Home at her mother's home. Instead, they invited her to the campus. Each of the thirty-eight children received gifts, pink and purple watches for the girls and radio headsets for the boys. Elizabeth also gave the home $400 that her staff had collected. The home planned to use it for sports equipment.

Several of the children and the volunteers there were confident the woman slicing the cake would be president. One child who had sung a song about a train for the secretary of transportation looked to the future when she said, "My gift is my song, but I'll be eighteen and I'll elect her."

The 1988 presidential election, and Elizabeth's role in it, was a big topic in 1987. Although Bob Dole had not made an official announcement, his intention to run was common knowledge. When Elizabeth had resigned from the Federal Trade Commission to help with his unsuccessful 1980 campaign, some women had been disappointed that she had put his career ahead of her own. Now many called on her to keep her cabinet post. From early 1987 she was under pressure both not to resign and to resign. Her assistant told a *Time* magazine reporter that when Bob suggested in January that she would have to resign eventually, "I've rarely seen her angry, but she was annoyed."

In 1987, Secretary Dole and Leader looked ahead to the 1988 presidential election. She left the cabinet to help with the campaign.

Elizabeth tried to do two jobs—run the Department of Transportation and campaign for her husband. In September the *Washington Post* reported that in August, a hot month when Congress goes home and the government slows down, Elizabeth had traveled eighteen days, seven of them on weekends. When a *Time* reporter asked Elizabeth about her campaign travel, she asked if there was a difference between a candidate and the spouse of a candidate retaining their jobs during a campaign.

She says, "I felt very strongly I had to stay through the summer to get a rule out on airplane delays. That summer was so awful. The public almost rose up because of the delays and the rest. This delay rule was important enough for me to go through that in order to get the rule out. That was not without cost to me. I was glad I did stay. The rule has made a difference. There was no way I could push it any faster."

She concludes, "You have to be sure a rule is going to stand up to appeal, and they are all appealed. If you don't have the right foundation and basics for it, if you rush it through without the proper legal care, you will lose it all."

In September Elizabeth resigned as secretary of transportation to devote full time to Bob's campaign. Part of that effort was finalizing a dual autobiography, *The Doles, Unlimited Partners,* written with Richard Norton Smith and published in early 1988.

The campaign began well, and Elizabeth received part of the credit for that. The *U.S. News and World Report* called Elizabeth "her husband's biggest asset."

In Iowa Bob won in every county. He took South Dakota, Minnesota, and Kansas. When Bob went into the crucial New Hampshire primary, his pollster told her he would defeat Vice-President Bush and probably win the Republican nomination. Instead, George Bush, with the help of Governor John Sununu, won in New Hampshire. Bob's campaign soon floundered.

For Elizabeth, at least one good thing came out of campaigning in New Hampshire. She took up skiing again. She enjoyed it so much she bought a pair of short skis, which are easier to use and to carry on planes than long ones.

Bob's daughter, who had her own campaign schedule, recalls her surprise at learning Elizabeth skied in front of network television cameras. "No way I would have done that," Robin says. "She's got a lot of daring. Doing that said a lot. She had to be willing to tumble down a hill on camera."

In Illinois the campaign suffered a small disaster. Bob had put a good part of his campaign funds there into producing a thirty-minute television program rather than broadcasting individual ads. Technical problems ruined the production, and the funds were lost. Elizabeth admired the way her husband accepted the setback. She says, "He was very calm. He was very gracious to everyone around him. He wasn't blaming anyone."

Although some of his remarks during the campaign itself had been bitter and he was unlikely to have another chance at the presidency, Bob came to joke about his defeat. More than a year later, speaking before the Republican National Committee, he said the night he withdrew from the presidential race he slept like a baby. His punch line: "Every two hours I woke up and cried."

As Bob's star faded, Elizabeth's burned bright. Many viewed her as a dark-horse possibility for vice-president. Syndicated columnist Ellen Goodman wrote that Elizabeth should be the Dole on the Republican ticket. Goodman said Elizabeth had a "squeaky reputation," which some of the men in the Reagan administration didn't, and would appeal to women. This was important because of the continuing political gender gap. She also had a record of achievement in government. Goodman wrote that she didn't know how Elizabeth would feel about running for vice-president with the man who had defeated her husband but concluded, "If the Republicans are smart, they'll offer it."

13

Working at Labor

Both the Doles made George Bush's list of possible vice-presidential candidates, but he named J. Danforth Quayle, an Indiana senator Elizabeth had helped campaign in 1986.

Elizabeth was very visible at the convention. She served as temporary chair and gave numerous interviews. One question frequently asked was how her husband would have felt if she had been on the ticket. She said he would "be very supportive of anything I would be involved with because that's the kind of man he is."

That fall Elizabeth once again rode the campaign trail during the presidential and congressional campaigns. George Bush and Dan Quayle defeated Michael Dukakis and Lloyd Bentsen, but the Democrats won the majority of the seats in both the House and the Senate. Bob became Senate minority leader.

Elizabeth had come to another critical point in her career. A number of law firms and corporate boards had approached her about positions, and she had been mentioned as a possible congressional candidate in North Carolina or appointee for another cabinet office. She delayed making a major decision on her future but signed on with a speakers' bureau. While at DOT, she had been one of the four or five most requested Republican speakers, receiving approximately 6,000 speaking invitations a year.

She used her unaccustomed leisure to read material that had nothing to do with transportation, set up a regular exercise program that included using a treadmill she had given Bob, catch up on neglected matters, and work with nephew John on a special project. They began to investigate the possibility of organizing a massive national bipartisan campaign to encourage Americans to give their "fair share" of money and time to help others. She was to discuss the idea privately but not publicly for almost two years.

Near the end of 1988, she mentioned her idea to the president-elect when he told her he wanted her to be part of his administration but did not specify a position. On December 21 she went to Salisbury to spend the holiday with her family. The next morning Bush called to ask her to become the secretary of labor, a department with approximately 18,500 employees and a budget of $31 billion.

She remembers, "Suddenly he gives me this concrete opportunity. I said, 'Let me think about it, because I've got to see if I feel a sense of mission. I need to know more about the Labor Department.' " Bush's office arranged to send voluminous material to her via a facsimile machine in a friend's office in Salisbury. At 9:00 P.M. he called Elizabeth to plead: "Tell Washington to stop." He had run out of fax paper and had to go buy more.

Then, Elizabeth says, "I started looking through all the things in the department, and I thought, 'My word, it is the people's department.' It seemed to me there's a lot that could be done. I saw that unemployment was very low, but minority youth unemployment was quite high."

Other issues that interested her included equal job opportunities for women, the changing work force, safety in the work place, discrimination, and pensions. She decided the "fair share" project could wait.

Her mother says simply, "She looked at it carefully, and when she saw . . . the day care and the dropouts, she took it. She said, 'Now that makes it worthwhile.' "

When Bob called, Elizabeth's mother asked him what he thought about his wife taking the job. According to the *Salisbury Post,* Bob's sympathetic mother-in-law said, "He told me it would be a fine thing if she doesn't let it consume her. I think that was a gentle hint. He doesn't want to be neglected."

Elizabeth's experience in education, the defense of poor inner-city clients, consumer advocacy, and safety gave her background on some of the issues the department dealt with. She also knew those with whom she would be working in and out of the government. She told a hometown reporter, Rose Post, "I think the key to a cabinet position is understanding Washington, knowing how the cabinet works, understanding the relationships and how to move the president's agenda forward—and knowing the players."

She also said she didn't plan to take work home. She laughs at herself for thinking that but says, "Bob and I talked about it, that we really wanted to have home as an oasis, so I'm much better about that."

She cut her normal office day down to about ten hours and said, "I take some things home, and he does, too, now and then. I tend to see what he's going to be up to. If I see him saying, 'I've really got to look at this homework,' then I feel, 'Okay, I'm going to get mine out.' "

For years they have relaxed by watching old movies together and by working out, first on an exercycle and later on a treadmill. "We both are fanatics now on exercise," she says. "Both of us use the treadmill every night that we're home."

She also says, "I remember when I used to feel I had to work seven days a week. I control that very well now. Sundays are *off limits.*"

Most Sundays she and Bob attend the Foundry Methodist Church on 16th Street approximately one mile north of the White

House. One winter morning they saw a man lying on the sidewalk as they went to church. After the service he was still there. Elizabeth went home, got two blankets, went back to the man, and began to spread them over him.

He roused himself and asked, "What time is it?"

She replied, "It's 1:30. It's so cold I brought you some blankets."

"I can't use blankets," he said. "I can't carry them."

She took the blankets and gave him some money. When she got home, she called her mother to tell her about the homeless man. Her mother said, "You did the wrong thing. That money will probably go for liquor."

"I can't help it," said Elizabeth. "I had to do something."

Her attitude toward the homeless wasn't new or limited to Sundays. She would continue to try to help them personally and through special programs at the Department of Labor and the Red Cross.

Elizabeth's appointment to the Department of Labor received considerable approval and little opposition. Some said she received the position because Bush wanted to please her husband and end the bitterness built up during the primaries. Such remarks saddened Elizabeth. She believed her record showed she had earned the appointment.

She began to prepare for her confirmation hearings—and the job. In addition to reading and talking to experts, she made a nine-city tour of job training sites. In mid-January, the *Washington Post* said she "is a voracious reader, famous for requesting backup information for her backup information. She has been holed up in the Labor Department, reading prodigiously, in preparation for confirmations hearings that are almost certain to be a love feast."

The prediction proved correct. In the hearing, which lasted little more than an hour, Elizabeth stressed her agreement with the president's position that the government should encourage, not require, business to offer such benefits as health insurance, child care, and parental leave. Any benefits Congress required should be aimed at low-income families.

She sounded a central theme, saying, "The mission of the Labor Department must be to coordinate a strategy of 'growth plus,' growth plus policies to help those for whom the jobs of the future are now out of reach because of a skills gap, family pressures, or because of a lack of supportive policies."

Elizabeth wanted to be sworn in at the Potomac Job Corps Center, but the president's security staff said it would be too difficult to make the area secure. Instead, the ceremony took place in Labor's Great Hall. This time Elizabeth asked a law school

Secretary Elizabeth Dole, President George Bush, Job Corps member Anthony Bond, Senator Bob Dole, and Judge Judith Rogers take part in the swearing-in ceremony.

classmate, District of Columbia Court of Appeals Chief Judge Judith W. Rogers, to swear her in and an outstanding Job Corps trainee, Anthony Bond, to hold the Bible. The Center's choir sang.

Soon Elizabeth was in the middle of a battle over raising the minimum wage, which had remained at $3.35 an hour throughout the eight years of Ronald Reagan's presidency. Democratic senators proposed raising it to $4.65 an hour over three years. President Bush threatened to veto the bill and insisted on a six-month training wage of $3.35 an hour for every new employee and raising the minimum wage per hour for others to $4.25. Elizabeth testified that raising the minimum wage to $4.65 would result in the loss of 650,000 jobs.

Much of labor and some of her early allies attacked the administration's stand. The National Women's Political Caucus pointed out that in 1989 it took $4.59 to buy what $3.35 would in 1981, that women were more than twice as likely as men to work for minimum wages, and that a woman working forty hours a week at minimum wage could not support a family of three above the poverty level. Nonetheless, after long hours of negotiation, the administration's bill passed.

Many of those who criticized Elizabeth for her stand on the minimum wage praised the steps she took to end one of the nation's most bitter strikes in years, that of the United Mine Workers against the Pittston Coal Company. A major issue was health care benefits for retired workers.

The strike began in early April. In October, with the union and company not even negotiating, Elizabeth went to see for herself what was going on. After her visit she said, "I saw families against families, brothers against brothers. This is tearing entire communities apart."

The next day she met in her office with the head of the union and the company's chairman. The two opponents had not met since the strike began, but she convinced them to let her appoint a mediator, a person acceptable to both sides.

"Her staff didn't want her to do it because they thought it would just bog down," says her mother. "But I think she handled it the right way. She got someone who was experienced and who was well liked."

The mediation continued the rest of the year, with the announcement of the settlement being made on New Year's Day. Mary Hanford has her own interpretation of why Elizabeth succeeded when failure seemed so likely. She says, "I think a woman can handle something that's emotional like that better than a man. A man can, well, he'll see about it tomorrow, sort of push it off."

Newspapers around the country praised the secretary of labor for her role in ending the strike and for her courage in taking a political risk. The *Washington Post* quoted an industry official as saying, "If she had lost, she wouldn't have been able to stay on as secretary of labor."

Elizabeth says, "That was a bit of a risk, but it was well worth taking. Let's say we hadn't succeeded. How could we really get in trouble for trying? Yet there are those who said to me, 'Yes, you would have been in deep trouble had you not succeeded.' "

An Associated Press article distributed to newspapers all over the country began, "Labor Secretary Elizabeth Dole may have made a philosophical homecoming when she put aside a decade of Republican labor doctrine and intervened in the Pittston Coal strike last fall."

Some union members and officials condemned Elizabeth and other administration officials for taking no action to end two other bitter, long-lasting strikes, those against Eastern Airlines and Greyhound Bus Lines.

Elizabeth pointed out that the regulations governing airlines would not permit government interference because other airlines were serving the public. "We had no option there," she says. As for the bus strike, the Labor Department could not act, she says, because "the parties were not in agreement to have mediation."

Library Resource Center
Renton Technical College
3000 NE 4th St.
Renton, WA 98056-4195

While the strikes were making headlines, Elizabeth was taking numerous other steps to bring about changes. She asked Congress to increase her budget for inspectors so she could improve enforcement of laws by the Occupational Health and Safety Administration. Labor began issuing new guidelines for preventing and treating crippling repetitive motion injuries, a particularly severe problem in the meat-packing industries.

Elizabeth proposed bigger fines for those who violated laws, including child labor laws. A massive surprise inspection in early 1990 showed that, with fewer young people to hire, more businesses were ignoring laws on working hours and conditions for teenagers.

Tackling a familiar safety problem, she proposed that all private industry employees be required to wear seat belts in motor vehicles and helmets on motorcycles while on the job. She estimated that obeying these rules would save 684 lives a year. The U.S. Chamber of Commerce objected to forcing the change, calling it "another example of regulatory overkill."

Changes in the governments of Eastern Europe brought international problems to the Department of Labor. The movement began in Poland, the first Eastern bloc country to do away with communism and its centrally controlled economy and try to establish a market economy, with private ownership and limited government control, similar to that in the United States.

In August 1989, Elizabeth and Bob went to Poland on a working vacation, arriving on the day the Polish people held their first free election in many years. They were trying to rebuild their economy to be more like the American and less like the Soviet system. Later she was part of a delegation of cabinet officials and business and labor leaders who went to Poland to find ways to provide training in business management and craft skills, set up an unemployment insurance system, and gather statistical information.

Elizabeth says, "I came back wanting to raise money to help Poland's people," but Labor Department lawyers said she couldn't approach any group, even a church, because of the department's regulatory role. A donation to Poland could be viewed as an attempt to influence a decision.

"At one point," says Elizabeth, "I was trying to help with infant formula. I did a certain amount of that before I was stopped. I said, 'Just take me off to jail for raising money for infant formula.'" She solved the problem of not being able to co-chair the bipartisan effort. "I got my husband to stand in for me. He can do it, but I can't."

She also found a way to ask for private assistance for Poland. She says, "We got the authority from Congress to do it. They wrote into the Poland legislation a little section that says, 'The Secretary of Labor is hereby authorized to solicit and receive gifts for Poland.'"

Elizabeth's interest in humanitarian matters attracted attention outside of government. In early 1990 an American Red Cross

The Doles met with earthquake victims in Armenia while delivering medical supplies from Project Hope there in 1989.

113

(ARC) representative called her. The organization's president had resigned in May 1989, and ARC was seeking a dynamic leader with experience in running a complex organization, strong communication skills, the ability to build a consensus and develop leaders, and the courage to make painful decisions. The caller asked if she would consider the position.

With vital new programs at Labor still on the drawing board and changes in old policies just beginning to be implemented, Elizabeth wanted to remain at her post. Still, cabinet posts don't last forever, and the ARC position interested her. She knew of the importance and scope of the work of the organization Clara Barton had founded to help victims of war and natural disasters in this country and to work with similar organizations around the world. Work by ARC during two recent crises, a hurricane and an earthquake, had brought it new national attention—and considerable criticism. Obviously the new president would face major problems.

Elizabeth agreed to talk to Marian Andersen, a Nebraskan who was head of ARC's selection committee and a member of its fifty-person policy-making body, the board of governors. The women found they had many views in common on the humanitarian and educational issues with which Red Cross staff and volunteers, including approximately 135,000 under eighteen years old, were dealing. Also, Andersen applauded Elizabeth's idea of encouraging Americans to increase their giving to those in need.

Nevertheless, Elizabeth told Andersen that the timing was wrong. The selection committee would have to choose from its many other candidates.

14

A Seat at the Table

One of Elizabeth's major concerns as secretary of labor was the nation's need for workers with skills to produce products and services that could compete in the world, not just the region or nation. To complicate matters, the rate at which new workers are becoming available is lower in the 1990s than at any time since World War II.

Ever an optimist, she saw these conditions serving to promote equal opportunity in jobs and society. To function efficiently, many businesses will have to change hiring and training practices. Speaking to the National Urban League in 1989, she said, "I firmly believe that we will not totally eliminate discrimination from our society until we have stamped it out of our economy."

Because the traditional source of new workers, white males, is limited, she said, "Those who have been outside looking in—many women, members of minorities, the disadvantaged, the disabled—will have unprecedented opportunities for productive work. . . . every man and woman who wants a job can have a job—if they have the skills."

She pointed out that the jobs of the 1990s demand better

reading, writing, math, and reasoning skills. More than half of these jobs require education beyond high school.

She said, "Unfortunately, there are a lot of young people out there who did not make the connection between success in school and success in the real world. There is a direct link—a profound link—between the two. Today's young people face many challenges, but they can be assured of good job, a fulfilling job, if they stick in there and get a good education."

The skills gap affects both young people looking for their first jobs and employees who must retrain for new jobs as the old ones disappear. To narrow the skills gap, she tried to bring together labor, private industry, education, and government.

Secretary Dole visits a Job Training Partnership Act trainee at the Fort Wayne (Indiana) Community Schools-Regional Vocational School.

Elizabeth sought amendments to the Job Training Partnership Act to target those "who are least skilled and most disadvantaged." In 1990 Labor began to test Youth Opportunities Unlimited, a program that assesses each participant to see what he or she needs, trains each person accordingly, and continues to provide assistance during the first year on the job.

Elizabeth also sought to involve business in helping at-risk young people. In March 1990, she told a meeting of the National Association of Manufacturers, "Today, I issue a challenge to each of you to involve at least 10 percent of your employees in some type of mentoring program with at-risk youth." She was to make like challenges in other speeches, and in private conversations, during and after her time at the Department of Labor.

She says, "I believe that the programs that work best, that provide the most benefit, that change the most lives, are programs involving mentoring—one-to-one relationships between at-risk youth and a caring role model."

She also encouraged development of apprenticeship and school-to-work programs. She says that successful school-to-work programs do four things: motivate students to stay in school, allow them to reach high academic achievements, link classroom learning to work-site experience and learning, and improve the chance of getting a good job.

She knew the working conditions of the 1950s, her teenage years, differed greatly from those facing today's teenagers. When Elizabeth finished high school and college, minorities, including women, had far fewer job options than they do today. The number of women professionals, such as doctors and lawyers, has doubled since 1972, and the number of women in managerial jobs has almost tripled. Nevertheless, in 1990 working women earned only 70 cents for each dollar earned by working men.

Speaking to a women's group in England, Elizabeth said, "There can be little doubt that a woman, no matter how well schooled, what her age, or how thick her portfolio of credentials, enters many business organizations with limited or no hope of reaching the top. The positions of power and decision-making in business are still held primarily by men. For example, of the 500 largest companies in America, just two—two out of 500—have a woman chief executive officer."

She foresees this glass ceiling, the invisible barrier preventing women and minorities from rising to high positions, gradually vanishing as they become essential to the work force.

To speed that up, she set up a program to check on whether companies are giving people a chance to move up. Elizabeth said, "What it does is look at qualified women and minorities who are in middle management jobs and are doing very well. Are they in the training programs? Are they being developed for higher positions? Are they on rotational assignments? What's the reward structure? You look at the kinds of things that companies do to develop people for the top positions and see whether those qualified women and minorities are involved in those activities. If they're not, you've got a problem." Of her own senior staff at Labor, well over half were women and minorities.

Elizabeth wanted her department to set an example in many ways, to be a model workplace. She called in a team from the Federal Quality Institute to advise on "trying to change the work place from being sort of the rigid, authoritarian, hand-down-the-orders to employee participation, a whole set of changes."

She ensured senior staff's participation in planning by taking them on a retreat—the method she had used with student government officers at Duke. She says, "I really believe in that. You get away from the telephones and all the day-to-day pressures. You have a chance to really think about and plan the future." They laid out goals and objectives and put them into a schedule called a timeline. She said, "I want these goals to be their goals. I don't want to hand them down and say, 'Here's what we're going to do, folks.'

Rather I want them to possess the goals, to own them because they fed into it."

Describing her day-to-day operation, Elizabeth said, "Every morning we have an 8:30 meeting with just my senior staff—my deputy and some of the key assistant secretaries. They go into a 9 o'clock session for thirty minutes that goes in a little deeper. They are beginning to implement what we decided.

"Then there is also a policy review board that meets on all major issues. I don't meet with them. Every other Friday there's the executive staff. They are very much involved in total quality management and how we can make the department a model."

She believes in giving her senior staff members a lot of responsibility. "To me the leader of the organization should be the person who has a vision, who feels committed. Once you have developed goals, you provide that vision, and, you hope, the inspiration."

To get the ideas and feelings of employees with whom she didn't work directly, Elizabeth went on walkabouts every two weeks or so. She walked into an office or the cafeteria and sat down to chat with employees about what interested them.

Cabinet members have a great deal, but not complete, independence. As Secretary of Labor Elizabeth Dole said, "The president has such a broad array of interests to be concerned about that you may fight for something internally that you think is very important. But as he looks at the overall picture, the timing isn't right for one reason or the other. Something else is going on that's going to conflict with that. I think you have to be willing to say, 'Okay, I am part of a bigger team here.' You may not always get approval for everything you want to do at that moment."

As one of the few women to rise to a cabinet position, Elizabeth urged women to seek power and use it for the good of the nation.

She said, "Many women coming up through the political route are very much involved in community organizations—school

boards, the churches, others. They develop a real sense of commit-
ment and dedication to good government. And somehow or other
the idea of exercising power, to some, is distasteful. It seems to run
counter to what has guided their conscience, their steps. I think that
attitude is changing, though, that women are beginning to realize
that they need a place at the table if they are going to be able to
reach those good goals, to make a difference to people. The positive
use of power is a good thing."

She stressed, "You've got to be able to have that seat at the table.
You are trying to reach those goals in a positive way, which means
exercising power."

In early 1990, *McCall's* magazine gave its readers the names of
five prominent women in politics and asked readers to vote for their
choice to be the first woman president. Elizabeth refused to give
the magazine an interview for the article, fearing that would be
interpreted as an intention to run. When readers made her the
number one choice, she still would not grant an interview. Instead
she gave the magazine this statement for its September 1990 issue:
"I am convinced that in my lifetime a woman will break through
the political glass ceiling and be elected president."

Not long after that, Marian Andersen, the head of ARC's
search committee, contacted Elizabeth again. "I happened to call
her the night before we were going to have the conference call
about one of the two people we were going to decide on to be the
new president of Red Cross," Andersen says. The conference call
was scheduled for 11:00 A.M. After more than a year of studying
some 200 candidates, the committee had promised the board of
governors they would be able to have a nominee for president by
the October meeting. Made up primarily of volunteers elected by
chapters around the country, the board comes together only twice
a year.

Andersen had given up hope that Elizabeth would leave her

"Labor of love," but, "I said to her a couple of times, 'I still think you're the perfect one.' "

Elizabeth slept little that night as she wondered what to do about this "now-or-never opportunity." Later, the decision made, she explained some of her considerations. Taking the Red Cross presidency was more a life-time than a night-time decision She traces its origins directly back to when, in writing *The Doles, Unlimited Partners,* she examined her life as never before. She realized then the major source of satisfaction in all her work had been meeting people's primary needs: organizing the conference on education of the deaf, defending the poor, protecting consumers, and promoting safety. As she worked at Labor to provide new opportunities, safe working conditions, and secure pension plans, the conviction grew that what she most wanted to do was to work on those issues "where people are vulnerable, where there's a real human need."

She says, "The Red Cross does that full time, and that's what made it so very attractive. It's really an opportunity to do what I love."

The Red Cross appealed to her for another reason: It could be the vehicle for encouraging people to give of their time and resources to meet a variety of needs. Marian Andersen, along with other members of the search committee, had supported the idea she had been developing since 1988. Elizabeth says, "It makes the Red Cross very attractive because there is an opportunity, a structure, in which that idea, that vision, could materialize, whereas otherwise I would have been starting in on my own from scratch."

On the other hand, she wasn't ready to leave the "people's department." She says, "Ideally it would have been nice to stay with the job longer and then have the Red Cross, because I loved that job, and my team was as congenial as any team I've ever put together."

Perhaps the argument that swayed her to accept the Red Cross offer was that she had reached her goals for 1990, had completed most of her mission. Two years, she says, "is a good period of time to be in a job. You've had a chance to really move forward your agenda and see everything reach a point where it will continue, as we feel it will. A lot of things had been completed, so that was a sense of satisfaction."

15

Good-bye to Government?

The morning after the restless night brought on by Elizabeth's conversation with Marian Andersen, the secretary of labor had a business breakfast with an old friend from her Harvard days. He noticed her fatigue, and she told him that she had stayed awake thinking about the offer from Red Cross. He was a good person to tell, for he also has been Andersen's long-time friend. After the breakfast he called the search committee head to ask if the decision on the presidency could be postponed.

With the hour for the conference call approaching, Andersen's immediate reaction was that she couldn't delay. But she and the committee decided the chance to get Elizabeth made it well worth waiting a few more days for a final decision. Andersen says, "She did not say yes definitively until she talked to the president."

Elizabeth discussed her resignation with President Bush while they were flying to North Carolina to campaign for Senator Jesse Helm's re-election. The decision remained a secret for almost two weeks.

Elizabeth took special precautions to keep the word from getting around at the Labor Department. Andersen says, "I'd call her secret hotline. You know, ring twice and if no one answers, hang up." (Elizabeth had a separate line on which senior staff, and selected others, could reach her whenever important matters came up.)

On Tuesday, October 23, 1990, the news leaked that Elizabeth had called AFL-CIO president Lane Kirkland to tell him she was resigning the next day—the ARC Board of Governors had just elected her president.

Caught by surprise, reporters speculated on why the only woman in the cabinet was also the first cabinet officer to resign. Most assumed she was leaving for political reasons. Many wrote that Elizabeth meant to use the prestigious job to build a base for running for senator or governor in North Carolina in 1992 or for national office later. With a budget of approximately a billion dollars, a staff of 23,000, approximately 2,700 chapters, and more than a million volunteers, the American Red Cross would give her the opportunity to prove her ability in running a large and complex organization.

What's more, she would remain in the public eye, for the Red Cross works in almost every American community in providing assistance after natural disasters, collecting blood from donors to distribute to hospitals and the armed services, and giving first aid and safety courses. Such visibility would be ideal for anyone with political ambitions, and Elizabeth Dole had proved herself an expert in making the most of media coverage.

Many journalists reported rumors that Elizabeth had been un-happy at the Department of Labor. The stories varied, but they included charges that the White House did not allow her to make decisions on policy matters, to set up new programs, to take the lead in getting legislation through Congress, or to receive recognition for her work. Some stories said that business had been displeased with her because she had stepped up enforcement of safety and health laws. Some stories said labor had been displeased with her because she had not intervened in the devastating Eastern Airlines and Greyhound Bus strikes and had not succeeded in persuading the White House to follow pro-labor policies.

Some who didn't know her saw another motivation for the resignation: Her salary at Red Cross probably would be approximately double the $98,400 she received as secretary of labor.

The morning after the story broke, Elizabeth and President Bush held a press conference to announce she would leave her government position in one month. President Bush expressed his regret at losing her and said she had "earned the respect of the American people."

Elizabeth thanked him for his faith in her and explained why she was leaving government after twenty-five years. "I have the opportunity to continue public service in a different way, as the president of the American Red Cross," she said. "I will join an army that includes more than a million volunteers in this country, more than 250 million around the world—those whose sole mission is to meet human needs, to improve the quality of human life."

She pointed out that the president, as honorary chairman of ARC, in a sense would still be her boss—and would be only two blocks away. Although she didn't mention it, several of her fellow cabinet officers, including the secretaries of state and of defense, serve as presidential appointees on the ARC Board of Governors.

In answering journalists' questions that day and later, Elizabeth dismissed most of their reports on why she had resigned. The question about her political plans she answered repeatedly, "I am not planning to run for anything." After all, to run for office in North Carolina in 1992, she would have had to move there to establish residency almost immediately. Concerning a national office, she noted that no one runs for the vice-presidency and "I have no plans to run for president." Many commented, however, that she didn't say she would *never* run for president.

As for having White House support for her programs, she has

said, "We were right in there on all the issues. The president was supportive of all the initiatives I wanted to go forward with. There was never a, 'No, we don't want to do that,' or 'Put that on hold.' " She cited her participation in presidential policy councils and cabinet meetings. "Our views were part of a meaningful discussion on a number of occasions. I felt it might have made a difference there."

After their press conference at the White House, Elizabeth called Labor employees into the Great Hall to tell them the news and to give her annual assessment of what they had accomplished. She spoke of her and their efforts "to improve the skills, safety, and security of American's workforce." She expressed a deep conviction: "The contributions of each of you matter. Everybody counts."

She said that everybody counts in another way, too. Everybody has the rights that Thomas Jefferson defined as "life, liberty, and the pursuit of happiness." That means, in part, she said, "a chance at a good education, a decent job, and a secure retirement. And, in return, all citizens would accept a responsibility to work hard, provide for their family, and obey the law." This she called a "social contract," one in danger of being broken.

The secretary of labor spoke of the challenges still to be met and issued a call she would echo as president of the American Red Cross: "But each of us must start with our own corner of the world. Each of us in this room and all across the nation must do what we can to ensure, that here in America, everybody does still count."

During the next few days, newspapers carried assessments of Elizabeth's work at the Department of Labor. Many noted that her achievements must be measured in terms of the possibilities in a Republican administration, for traditionally Republicans favor business rather than labor.

Some gave her higher marks for effort than for results. For example, a headline in the October 25 *New York Times* read, "Departing Labor Secretary Is Hailed For Intent, but Role Hindered

Action." Reporter Peter T. Kilborn quoted AFL-CIO's Lane Kirkland as saying Elizabeth "did her best to represent the working people and their unions in a Republican administration." Kilborn also wrote that Senator Edward M. Kennedy, the Democrat chairing the Labor committee, praised her and said, "It cannot have been easy serving as a pro-labor Secretary in an anti-labor Administration."

Some newspapers carried little but praise. An editorial in the *Boston Globe* said the administration "has lost one of its classiest members. Her firm sense of purpose, combined with a strong sense of the need to be politic in the pursuit of improved conditions for those under her responsibility, restored dignity and forcefulness to an office that had suffered badly during the Reagan administration."

A *Dallas Times Herald* headline read, "Dole did well at Labor Dept." The editorial called her "one of the most distinguished women ever to serve in government" and stated "she did an excellent job on a variety of fronts."

In her hometown, the *Salisbury Post* pursued the story diligently. The day Elizabeth resigned, reporter Rose Post interviewed Betty Dan Gilliam, the lifelong friend who had predicted Liddy would grow up to be president. Betty Dan said, "I really don't think she's as interested in her career as she is in making a difference in lives. I think for her that it's almost like fulfilling a calling, that she can make a difference in the lives of other people and in the world, rather than in any political gains that she might make."

The next day *Post* staff members who had known and covered Elizabeth for years discussed what they had learned from their own and others' interviews. The subsequent editorial concluded that reports on Elizabeth's political ambitions and her frustration with being outside the administration's inner circle might have some basis. "But there's also the possibility, however remote it may seem in this cynical age, that Mrs. Dole means exactly what she says."

The editorial continued, "Maybe there's no hidden agenda.

Maybe she really is fed up with the pressures and hypocrisies of modern American politics and longs for something more spiritually nourishing."

Referring to past and present press coverage, the *Post* said, "Media interviewers and others sometimes find her ever-upbeat, optimistic exterior a little too goody-goody to be true, but maybe that's the real Liddy."

In her last month at the Department of Labor, Elizabeth pushed hard to finalize various programs. One of those of great personal concern to her was restructuring job training programs for homeless persons. As in her programs to train at-risk youth, she adopted a holistic, or comprehensive, strategy for each person.

In announcing the program she said, "We must help the homeless find a permanent solution, so they do not continue spinning through the revolving door of emergency assistance. This initiative is designed to provide the homeless with more than a place to sleep. Many of our homeless desperately need basic skills training, literacy, remedial education, drug counseling. How else will we break the cycle of homelessness and emergency assistance, and arm these Americans not just with a temporary roof and a meal, but with the independence and skills for a lifetime of productive work?" She and the secretary of housing and urban development signed an agreement that his department would assist in providing both short-term and permanent housing for the homeless whom the Labor Department is training.

Marian Andersen—like many before her—began to worry about the long hours Elizabeth puts in. Andersen said to Joan Warren, a Red Cross friend from Detroit, "I wonder when she has time to relax."

Warren replied, "Don't you see? Working *is* her fun."

During the break between jobs, Elizabeth took some time to relax—and learn about her new responsibilities—in Salisbury. She and her mother updated her scrapbooks. Elizabeth insisted that good and bad comments go in, but she took particular pleasure in documenting her good relations with both business and labor. She felt special pride in the trust and exchange of ideas she had established with organized labor.

She gave prominent place to two awards she received from organized labor in 1990, the Labor Management Award from the Work in America Institute and Construction Person of the Year from the AFL-CIO Building and Construction Trades Department. The scrapbook displays the introduction Robert A. Georgine, president of the AFL-CIO department, gave at the award dinner. It reads, in part, "Secretary Dole is a person who listens carefully to your requests, points of view, criticism or goals, and then levels with you about what she really will or will not do. This is not an attribute that is common in Washington. She is a friend of organized labor."

When Elizabeth became president of the American Red Cross in February 1991, the 110-year-old organization had been struggling to readjust to changing circumstances and needs for at least a decade. In the early 1980s, it had reorganized to give the 2,700 field units more independence in conducting programs. Throughout the decade the competition for volunteers and donations stiffened. In 1989 the Red Cross had received bad marks for its handling of two major disasters, a hurricane on the East Coast in September and an earthquake on the West Coast in October. In 1990 the Food and Drug Administration questioned the safety of the organization's massive blood services (blood donation and distribution) operation.

Before Elizabeth accepted the presidency, the chairman of the Board of Governors assured her that Red Cross was taking action to solve both problems. After a lengthy study, ARC had developed a long-term plan for the 1990s called Service Delivery 21 (SD21). As Elizabeth crammed for the new position, she realized the work had only begun.

Marian Andersen said, "We are looking at a strategic plan for the 21st century that may involve some radical departures from the

129

way the Red Cross does business. But I feel strongly that any organization worth its salt has to keep changing to remain true to its original mission or updated mission. I think Elizabeth will have the vision to work, to battle on."

Elizabeth began her new job by speaking to a gathering of ARC national staff. She said, "I've thought about how I wanted to get the message out that it is the volunteers who are the heart and soul of the Red Cross. And I decided that the best way I can let volunteers know of their importance is to be one of them. . . . Therefore, during my first year as president, I will accept no salary. I, too, will be a volunteer."

Bob had tried to talk her out of this sacrifice. As he told a reporter, "I thought she had a right to be paid." Elizabeth faced a crisis immediately. In mid-January, the Persian Gulf Conflict had begun. American troops, in cooperation with forces from other nations, were fighting to drive the Iraqi army from Kuwait. ARC had been debating a SD21 proposal to cut back on its traditional assistance to members of the armed forces and their families. Elizabeth and the organization decided ARC must continue to meet the needs of soldiers and their families. She announced a drive to raise $30 million.

When the war came to a quick end, she made an exhausting five-day trip to Saudi Arabia and Kuwait to deliver a million dollars worth of supplies, meet with Red Cross staff there, and study the needs for continued assistance to Americans and to the local population.

One of her most disturbing visits was to a Kuwaiti hospital for disabled children and elderly adults. During the occupation and war, the staff had fallen from 225 to 20, and 170 of the 700 patients had died from lack of care. Elizabeth and the reporter covering her visit left with tears on their cheeks, but not before Elizabeth had promised the few remaining nurses she would send volunteers to help them for a few weeks or months.

Before she left the Gulf, Elizabeth started to make calls. One went to an old friend in Salisbury, a recently retired pediatrician whose mother had served as a Red Cross nurse in World War I. He, his daughter, and two others from Elizabeth's hometown became part of the 42-member medical team that went to the hospital. American Red Cross volunteers also were helping Kurds who fled to the mountains and other Iraqis who fled to the desert to escape Saddam Hussein's army.

Elizabeth continued the fundraising campaign. While chapters

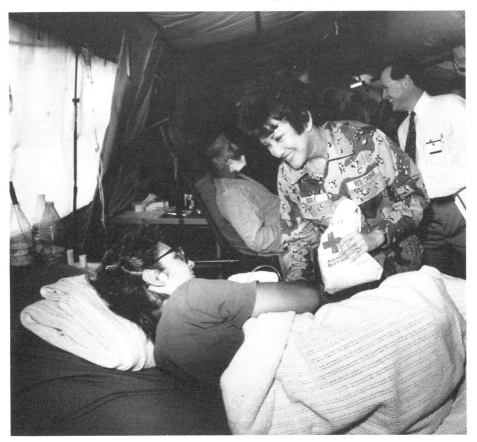

Elizabeth greets an American soldier in a hospital in Dhahran, Saudi Arabia, shortly after the Persian Gulf Conflict.

got donations from their communities, Elizabeth took primary responsibility for coaxing large corporations and other major donors to contribute. One of the contributors was singer Whitney Houston, who gave the royalties from her popular recording of the national anthem. Houston also became an at-large member of the governing board. Some corporations contributed their products or services. For example, airlines gave free flights to relatives going to visit wounded soldiers.

Frequently working into the night, Elizabeth coped with many other problems. One of the most urgent was ensuring a safe blood supply in the face of possible new variations of the virus causing AIDS and of charges some of the fifty-three blood centers had not taken sufficient care in handling blood. It was clear that the computer systems testing the blood needed replacement. Elizabeth declared, "We are going to make blood as safe as we can make it, or we stop collecting."

She talked with Jeffrey McCullough, the doctor who had come to Red Cross a few months before to strengthen blood services. Elizabeth recalls, "I asked, 'Do you think there might be six, seven, eight [centers] that need to be shut down?' He thought about it and said, 'No, it's not that there are a few that are weaker. The problems that we have are inherent throughout the system. It's a matter of having so many labs with so many computer systems.' "

Elizabeth says, "We were still trying to patch a fifty-year old system." They reached a major decision: ARC must shut down all blood centers and change the entire system—and still supply half the nation's blood.

They needed to move quickly. They had no time for the lengthy consultation process that both the organization and Elizabeth have favored in making decisions. The doctor took the lead in developing the operational plan. Elizabeth devised a strategy for getting government and board approval of the "transformation."

She asked the White House, the secretary of health and human services, the head of FDA, and the chair of the House Energy and Commerce Committee to speak with her confidentially. She says, "I explained what the situation was, that this was bigger than the Red Cross, that I was willing to do whatever they felt was necessary to meet the concerns that the government would have, and that I would also go to my board and ask for the money to do it. But I had to know that we could work together on this." She received their support. A critical element was FDA's agreement to work with ARC in designing the new system and in making prompt inspections so labs could reopen as quickly as possible. Delays could cost millions.

Just before the ARC national conference in May, Elizabeth and McCullough unveiled a plan to: close each blood center for eight weeks in order to bring in new equipment and train the staff; do all testing in ten new regional centers; set up one computer system; make specialized services available to small hospitals; and establish oversight boards for blood services, which had been under chapter boards. Elizabeth asked for $120 million over two-and-a-half years. ARC would have to borrow much of that from its special funds and from banks. In spite of the high cost, first the biomedical and financial committees and then the board approved the transformation unanimously.

Elizabeth says, "This is not anywhere close to being risk free, but you have to take some bold actions in life." Failure would mean hard times for the national blood supply, ARC, and her. She says, "It puts you way out there if it doesn't work." She also says, "It's one of the most important things I've ever done."

After the conference Elizabeth went home to celebrate her mother's ninetieth birthday. Elizabeth and John honored their mother for her lifetime of volunteerism by establishing the Mary Cathey Hanford Endowment Plan for At-Risk Youth through the Rowan County ARC chapter. The plan's purpose is "to provide at-risk youth an opportunity to enrich their community and their own lives." Teenagers work as paid interns to assist the chapter and the community. Mentors work with them, as do tutors from local colleges. Outstanding interns receive college scholarships.

Elizabeth says, "We thought about at-risk youth because she related so to it when it was one of my priorities at Labor."

Back at headquarters, Elizabeth began wrestling with another major issue, modernizing ARC's disaster services. In July the national office sent chapters a report detailing inadequacies revealed during 1989 disasters and outlining a revitalization plan to overcome these. It seeks to improve preparedness, delivery, capacity to meet the special needs of minorities, and communication among ARC units, the victims, the public, and local agencies.

A brief section pointed to disturbing trends: the difficulty in raising funds and recruiting volunteers, and the increasing needs of victims. One particular statement reflected Elizabeth's thinking: "Some of these trends, such as the growing number of homeless among disaster victims, may require the Red Cross to reexamine its traditional mix of services. But this and other broad issues go beyond the capacity of the Red Cross to address alone. They must be solved through a collaborative effort of all the governmental, non-profit, and private agencies which constitute our domestic disaster response system."

As with blood services, she concluded that more than patching would be needed to enable Red Cross to give "services relevant to the 1990s and beyond."

Much of Elizabeth's work at ARC deals with managing 23,000 staff members, most of them scattered around the country, in a time of change. In her first six months Elizabeth surveyed staff members for their opinions on the best way to reorganize the staff and used the results to make a new plan. She created a new office to work closely with field staff. She also set up mechanisms for improving financial control and accountability.

She said, "My bottom line is that I want to empower the chapters to be able to provide the services they feel are important in their communities. I want to ensure that when the Red Cross makes a pledge that it's going to do something, that we provide that service as efficiently and effectively as we can—and with culturally diverse teams of people. That's one of my top priorities." She and her staff also began to look for ways to increase the number of teenage volunteers in 1992, the seventy-fifth anniversary of the Junior Red Cross.

While her experience in government has proved of great value at the ARC, she realized almost immediately that heading a service organization is not the same as being a cabinet secretary. "It's a different structure altogether," she says. "You are involved in a lot of meetings. . . . It's a very thorough process of consensus building. That makes it a different sort of climate. I'm a great believer in consulting affected parties and constituent groups, but this is a more extensive process than I've had in the past."

She notes another difference: "On the philanthropic side, a lot of time is spent raising funds . . . from individuals, from foundations, from corporations and so on, whereas in government you are working with the Office of Management and Budget, the White House, and then Congress for the appropriations you need. One other difference is that instead of carrying forward the policies of the president . . . an executive in the nonprofit sector has to work to inform the board, to advise, to recommend, and then carry forward the policies of the board. And to make management decisions. The scope of responsibilities and obligations of nonprofits like Red Cross is so large that a great deal of your executive management is called for on a daily basis."

Elizabeth notes that management expert Peter Drucker has written that nonprofits need effective leadership and management a good deal more than businesses do.

Speaking of her switch from government to ARC she says, "It certainly meets my expectations of work that is very rewarding, very meaningful, very fulfilling."

Many wonder how long Elizabeth will feel that way, will want to apply her extraordinary intelligence, energy, and charm to the old humanitarian organization as it struggles to chart a new path. Will she soon return to government as an appointed or an elected official? During her government career, she stayed at agencies from fewer than two to little more than five years—normal terms for people in those positions. She left to move up or to help her husband campaign for national office.

Born in 1923, Senator Dole is unlikely to run for the presidency again. Born in 1936, Elizabeth could remain a dark-horse candidate for the presidency or the vice-presidency until after the turn of the century.

She firmly denied plans to run when she resigned as secretary of labor, but she knows well the unpredictability of political life. Also, she has found ground-breaking opportunities hard to resist, partly because they represent an advancement for women in general, not just herself.

She has said that, considering her experience and love for people, "It would not be unusual to find yourself running for an elected office."

At least part of her family doesn't expect her to run. Her mother calls the presidency "a terrible responsibility." Nephew John says, "I'm not sure that she is inclined to mount a campaign. I'm sure that there will be people urging her. In terms of her own initiative, deciding 'I'm going to run for this,' my guess is that won't happen. I think what could happen would be for her to be drafted as vice-president."

Elizabeth Hanford Dole may not know exactly where her drummer will lead her, but she knows well the beat to follow.

Chronology

1936—Mary Elizabeth Alexander Hanford born in Salisbury, North Carolina, to Mary and John Van Hanford.

1954—Graduated with high honors from Boyden High School, Salisbury; entered Duke University, Durham, North Carolina.

1957—Elected president of Women's Student Government Association at Duke University.

1958—Graduated from Duke University with a bachelor's degree in political science—honors included Student Leader of the Year, Phi Beta Kappa, and May Queen.

Moved to Boston area; became secretary to the head librarian, Harvard Law School Library, Cambridge, Massachusetts.

1960—Received Master of Arts in Teaching degree with joint major in government from Harvard School of Education.

1962—Entered Harvard Law School.

1965—Graduated from Harvard Law School; finalist for White House Fellowship.

1966—Became the coordinator of a national conference on education of the deaf at the Department of Health, Education, and Welfare, Washington, D.C.

1967—Defended impoverished defendants in District of Columbia courts as a community service.

1968—Got position in White House office of consumer affairs.

1969—Received promotion to deputy director of President's Committee on Consumer Interests.

1970—Named Outstanding Young Woman of the Year in Washington, D.C.

1973—Appointed as a Federal Trade Commission commissioner by President Richard M. Nixon.

1974—Named one of 200 of the nation's young leaders by *Time* magazine.

1975—Married Robert Joseph Dole, Republican senator from Kansas.

1976—Bob Dole nominated as Republican candidate for vice-president; Elizabeth took leave of absence to campaign for him and his running mate, President Gerald R. Ford.

1979—Resigned from the Federal Trade Commission to help her husband campaign for the Republican presidential nomination.

1980—Appointed by President-elect Ronald Reagan as director of his transition team's human services group.

1981—Appointed head of the White House Office of Public Liaison by President Reagan.

1983—Appointed secretary of transportation by President Reagan.

1984—Gave a major address at the Republican convention; Bob elected Senate majority leader; the Doles adopt miniature schnauzer, Leader.

1987—Resigned to help her husband campaign for the Republican presidential nomination.

1988—Publication of dual autobiography, *The Doles, Unlimited Partners*.

1989—Appointed secretary of labor by President George Bush. Received the National Safety Council's Distinguished Service to Safety Award.

1990—Received Labor Management Award from Work Institute of America and Construction Person of the Year Award from the AFL-CIO Building and Construction Trades Department; received the Sara Lee Frontrunner-Government award (a $10,000 contribution to a not-for-profit women's organization); received the Director's Choice Excellence in Leadership Award of the National Women's Economic Alliance.

Resigned as secretary of labor; elected president of the American Red Cross.

1991—Became president of the American Red Cross.

Further Reading

Dole, Bob and Elizabeth, with Richard Norton Smith. *The Doles, Unlimited Partners.* New York: Simon and Schuster, 1988.

Hamilton, Leni. *Clara Barton.* New York: Chelsea House Publishers, 1988.

Ross, Ishbel. *Angel of the Battlefield, The Life of Clara Barton.* New York: Harper & Brothers, 1956.

Index

About the Author

Carolyn Mulford has written books for both children and adults. She has been a magazine and newsletter writer and editor in the Washington, D.C., area for more than twenty years. A former Peace Corps volunteer and United Nations staff member, she loves to travel and has visited more than sixty-five countries.

973 .92092 MULFORD 1992

Mulford, Carolyn.

Elizabeth Dole, public
 servant

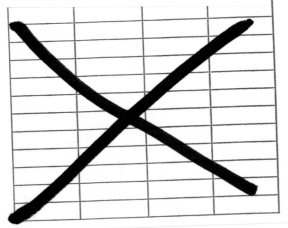

Library Resource Center
Renton Technical College
3000 NE 4th St.
Renton, WA 98056-4195